D1177417

CHAMPION OF WORLD PEACE

Dag Hammarskjold

BORN: July 29, 1905
DIED: September 18, 1961

The United Nations immediately brings to mind Dag Hammarskjold who picked up the threads of a strife-torn, faction-riddled UN and molded it into a powerful organization for world peace. He grew up in an atmosphere of politics and diplomacy and pursued his career from statesman to Secretary-General of the UN, never once losing sight of his ultimate goal—the preservation of world peace. The author brings to the book a perceptive delineation of a great man, and a skillful study of current world history that brings better understanding to some of the turbulent affairs of the present.

Books by I. E. Levine

BEHIND THE SILKEN CURTAIN
The Story of Townsend Harris

CHAMPION OF WORLD PEACE
Dag Hammarskjold

CONQUEROR OF SMALLPOX
Dr. Edward Jenner

ELECTRONICS PIONEER
Lee DeForest

INVENTIVE WIZARD
George Westinghouse

MIRACLE MAN OF PRINTING
Ottmar Mergenthaler

YOUNG MAN IN THE WHITE HOUSE
John Fitzgerald Kennedy

CHAMPION OF WORLD PEACE

DAG HAMMARSKJOLD

By I. E. Levine

JULIAN MESSNER

NEW YORK

Published by Julian Messner
Division of Pocket Books, Inc.
8 West 40 Street, New York 10018

© Copyright 1962 by I. E. Levine

Sixth Printing, 1965

Printed in the United States of America
Library of Congress Catalog Card No. 62-15418

To Delores and Gerald

CONTENTS

Chapter One

FLIGHT TO NDOLA

On the afternoon of September 17, 1961, a white, four-motored transport stood waiting near the terminal of Ndjili Airport outside of Léopoldville. As the plane's fuselage caught the rays of the orange African sun it looked for all the world like a giant tropical bird poised gracefully with wings outstretched. Off in the distance, beyond the tree-lined streets of the Congo capital, clouds cast eerie shadows on the murky waters of the mighty Congo River as it snaked its way through the jungles and grasslands of the great equatorial plateau.

Shortly after four o'clock, nine men and a woman emerged from the terminal building and silently made their way to the waiting aircraft, accompanied by a flight crew of six men. While the plane was being checked and fueled, the passengers huddled together in small clusters, conferring in low, guarded tones. One of the party, a slightly built, sandy-haired man in his fifties, stood off from the others, seemingly lost in his own thoughts. Occasionally, someone came up to him to whisper something, and at such moments his deeply etched face relaxed as he nodded or shook his head in quick, decisive reply. But then his bushy eyebrows furrowed together once more as he returned to his silent contemplation.

For Dag Hammarskjold, Secretary-General of the United Nations, there was indeed a good deal to think about as he waited to board his specially chartered plane at Ndjili Airport that September afternoon. His mission was one that reflected the grave concern of the entire world, and he was only too well

9

aware that at this particular moment in history the lives of thousands of men, women and children in this far-off tropical land rested on his slender shoulders. He knew, too, that his success or failure in this remote corner of civilization might eventually affect the lives of millions in all the other nations of the earth.

Yet his most immediate worry had to do with the dangers of the flight itself. The trip on which he and his party of aides and security officers were about to embark was hardly a routine one. It would take them a thousand miles southeast, over the very heart of the strife-torn Katanga Province of the infant Republic of the Congo, where even at that moment bloody fighting was taking place and scores were being killed and wounded.

There was good reason to be apprehensive. That morning, the white DC-6B chartered by the United Nations from the Swedish Transair Company had taken off from Elisabethville, capital of Katanga, amid a hail of bullets. One of its exhausts had been shot out, necessitating repairs and a careful check of the engines when it landed in Léopoldville. Moreover, reports had been received about a marauding Katanga jet fighter, known as "The Lone Ranger," who had been strafing United Nations garrisons and terrorizing UN aircraft and commercial flights in the Katanga area.

It was not his own safety that concerned Dag Hammarskjold. He had been shot at before, and in such matters he often took a fatalistic view of things. It was the welfare of the others in his party that gave him reason for concern. In addition to himself, the group of ten consisted of four United Nations aides, including one woman, a secretary; two UN security officers; a UN investigator; and two Swedish soldiers, normally stationed in Léopoldville, who were assigned to accompany him on this mission. In addition, there was the Swedish flight crew of six, and for these brave men, too, he felt a grave sense of responsibility.

It was for these reasons that the Secretary-General had taken elaborate precautions to keep the details of the flight a secret. Back at his temporary headquarters on the sixth floor of Le

Royale Building in Léopoldville, he had called in the members of his party and briefed them carefully. They would take off from Ndjili in late afternoon, he had told them, and the flight plan would include a detour that would bring the plane within the Katanga danger zone and the range of "The Lone Ranger" jet fighter after dark. The pilot of the transport, a veteran flier named Per Hallonquist, had been ordered to maintain strict radio silence all the way. What's more, Dag Hammarskjold had told them, fifteen airfields throughout the Congo and Rhodesia had been quietly alerted to stand by in case an emergency landing became necessary.

A few minutes before five o'clock the pilot and his crew completed their ground check of the huge plane and reported that it was ready for flight. The Secretary-General and his party climbed aboard, carrying their dispatch cases and hand luggage.

Up front in the cockpit Captain Hallonquist scanned his instrument panel for the last time, nodded to his copilot and reached for the throttles. One by one the huge motors roared to life. The backwash of the propellers cut through the hot, humid Congo air like a knife, and the airplane shuddered from the suppressed fury of the powerful engines. The craft taxied to the end of the field, turned onto the runway, where it seemed to pause momentarily like a runner getting his second wind, and began to move down the long airstrip, picking up speed. Faster and faster it raced until slowly it rose off the ground like a giant weighted bird and began to climb steadily, heading southeast.

Dag Hammarskjold and his party were headed for Ndola, in Northern Rhodesia, a small town near the border that separated Rhodesia from the Republic of the Congo. There, in neutral territory less than a hundred miles from the fighting in Katanga, the Secretary-General was to meet Moise Tshombe, leader of the secessionist province, in the hope that they could arrange a cease-fire between the Katanga forces and United Nations troops stationed there.

Dag Hammarskjold's decision to fly to Ndola had been made only a few days before, yet the events that led up to it had had their roots in a complicated sequence of earlier occurrences, a train of tragic events that went back more than fifteen months.

For three quarters of a century the Congo had been under the rule of Belgium. In 1885, as a result of explorations by Sir Henry M. Stanley, the Congo Free State was formed, with Leopold II of Belgium as the ruler and sole owner. In 1908, the Congo became a Belgian colony. Cruelly exploited by successive colonial administrations, the Congolese agitated for self-rule for decades, and finally, in the spring of 1960, the Belgian government announced it was pulling out of the Congo permanently. A new native government was established. Unprepared by the Belgians for self-rule and lacking trained administrators, the infant nation was torn apart from the start by rival political factions which were encouraged by foreign advisers and mercenaries serving in the armed forces.

To guarantee the peaceful settlement of Congolese problems, the United Nations had sent troops into the strife-ridden land. As a result, a measure of temporary stability had been achieved. Furthermore, to eliminate outside interference, the UN Security Council had passed a resolution on February 21, 1961, calling for the expulsion of the foreign troublemakers, many of whom were formerly with the Belgian colonial administration.

The central Congo government in Léopoldville had tried to comply with the United Nations order, but a thousand miles to the southeast, in the mineral rich province of Katanga, Belgian influence was still strong. There was bitter opposition to unification with the new central government, and the Katanga leaders refused to obey the United Nations directive. When the president of the central government saw that he could not enforce the expulsion decree in Katanga, he called for United Nations assistance. Immediately officials in the Katanga provincial government issued false announcements designed to terrify the population and stir up the native tribes. They warned that the United Nations was planning to disarm the Katanga armed forces and that soldiers from the central government in Léopoldville were on their way in United Nations planes to occupy the province by force.

In spite of attempts by the United Nations to deny the false reports and calm the Katanganese, the fear campaign succeeded. Led by foreign mercenaries, armed patrols of Katanganese menaced United Nations personnel. The tension mounted. On September 11, the United Nations deputy representative in Elisabethville was arrested on orders of a non-Congolese officer of the Katanga political police. Simultaneously arms were distributed by the Katanga officials to the populace. A United Nations garage was set on fire, and when UN troops attempted to fight the flames, the mercenaries began shooting at them and ordered attacks by the native patrols under their command. To protect themselves the United Nations soldiers began shooting back, and the casualties mounted. Almost a score of UN troops were killed in the fighting.

Meanwhile, the troubles in the Congo were having repercussions five thousand miles away. Just a few days before the outbreak of violence in Katanga, Dag Hammarskjold sat in his office on the thirty-eighth floor of the United Nations Building in New York City, frowning as he studied accounts of mounting tension in the Congo Province. In addition to the reports there was a letter from Prime Minister Cyrille Adoula of the Republic of the Congo inviting him to fly to Léopoldville at once to discuss United Nations aid to the infant nation. A flight to Africa at the moment would be difficult, for the opening of the annual UN General Assembly meeting was scheduled to take place in a matter of days. Yet he knew, too, that the growing trouble in Katanga might lead to a blood bath if it were not dealt with immediately.

It took the Secretary-General only a few seconds to make up his mind. He flicked the switch on his interphone, called his secretary and instructed her to make arrangements for an immediate flight to Léopoldville.

The plane left New York on September 12. When Dag Hammarskjold and his aides stepped off at Ndjili Airport many hours later they were greeted with the news that fighting had broken out between the mercenary-led Katanga forces and United Nations troops in Elisabethville.

For the next few days vain attempts were made to initiate discussions with Moise Tshombe, President of the Katanga Province. Finally, a message got through, and Tshombe agreed to meet with the Secretary-General on September 17 at Ndola, in neutral Rhodesian territory.

The chartered plane carrying Dag Hammarskjold and his United Nations party to the Ndola rendezvous had taken off from Léopoldville at five o'clock in the afternoon, and it was scheduled to land at Ndola before midnight. Moise Tshombe arrived at the Ndola airstrip in late afternoon, but he decided to wait there for the United Nations plane.

Shortly before eleven o'clock a plane bearing Lord Lansdowne, British Parliamentary Undersecretary of State for Foreign Affairs, who had agreed to act as intermediary at the ceasefire meeting, touched down at the tiny field. Newsmen who had learned of the scheduled meeting and had come to Ndola to cover it mistook the Englishman's plane for Dag Hammarskjold's and, without checking their facts, carelessly sent out a bulletin that the United Nations team had landed on schedule. Meanwhile Tshombe and Lord Lansdowne waited for the Hammarskjold plane for another half hour before leaving the airport to get some rest.

Shortly after 1:00 A.M. the control tower at Ndola got a message from a mysterious craft that refused to identify itself, asking permission to drop to six thousand feet. When nothing more was heard from the plane, the Ndola controller assumed it had veered away and landed at another field.

As the night wore on and there were no further reports, apprehension mounted in Ndola. In the early morning hours the Ndola police station received a report that a great flash in the sky had been noted sometime after midnight. All available information was relayed to the United Nations base headquarters in Léopoldville.

Deciding not to wait any longer, the UN officials in the Congo capital immediately ordered the organization of search and rescue parties and requested assistance from the Léopoldville embassies of several countries so that every available plane in the region could be used for the search. At the same time they released a public announcement that the plane carrying the Secretary-General of the United Nations was missing.

Back in United Nations headquarters in New York City, the news of the missing aircraft clattered into the cable room on the thirty-eighth floor, and shocked secretariat officials made a mad rush for the teletypes. Hour after hour they hovered over the machines, hoping for a scrap of information that would indicate that their boss was safe.

By now, too, newspapers and radio and television stations in all countries were carrying bulletins about the missing plane, and an anxious world waited for additional news. For people everywhere the critical hours of uncertainty led to questioning and wonder about this man Dag Hammarskjold. In his eight years of service as Secretary-General of the United Nations he had scrupulously shunned personal publicity, preferring to occupy a role of anonymity whenever possible. Indeed, in the eyes of the world he had become the very symbol of the United Nations, and millions of men, women and children found it difficult to attribute to him the characteristics of individual personality. But now, for perhaps the first time, people began to think of Dag Hammarskjold, not as an organizational symbol, but as a human being, and they began to ask themselves: What sort of man was he?

Chapter Two

THE BOY

They named him Dag, which means day.

He was born in Jönköping, a city in south central Sweden, on July 29, 1905. His parents had him christened Dag Hjalmar Agne Carl Hammarskjold, but even as a boy he felt the full name was too pretentious and liked to be known simply as Dag. Although the Hammarskjold family did not remain in Jönköping, summers and holidays continued to be spent in the family castle there, on the southern tip of Lake Vättern.

Dag's most cherished memories were of winter vacations at the lake and of how the dancing icecaps appeared and disappeared when the cold wind blew across the water. On such days there would be a warm fire crackling on the hearth, and it gave him a feeling of security to stare out the window at the icy blackness of the foaming waves. How different it was from summer when the warm yellow sun seemed to change the color of the lake to a crystal green. But summer or winter, he loved Lake Vättern.

He loved also the ancient stone walls of the Hammarskjold castle and the twisting stairways and the great halls where once the famous knights and nobles of Sweden gathered to pay their respects to his ancestors. On the walls were the weapons that the early Hammarskjolds had carried with them into battle, and it stirred him deeply to think that those carefully wrought swords and muskets and pikes had helped to weld a nation together.

Indeed, the story of the Hammarskjold family was inextricably woven into the history of modern Sweden. It began in 1610 when a cavalry captain was knighted by a grateful Swedish king as a reward for service to the crown and given the family name Hammarskjold which meant "hammer shield." During the next three centuries the Hammarskjold family became an important part of the Swedish aristocracy. They were not the ancient nobility and landed gentry who had fought bitterly against the crown over the issue of who would rule Sweden, but part of a new aristocracy, founded by the king himself. These were the families who had served the crown faithfully in its early efforts to unify Sweden, families dedicated to a concept of service to the kingdom.

Duty to family and country, hard work, loyalty to the crown —these became the guiding principles of the "civil service" aristocracy to which the Hammarskjold family proudly belonged They were the professional soldiers who formed the backbone of the Swedish army and the career officials who administered the government. For three hundred years, generations of Hammarskjolds had perpetuated the tradition by serving as military officers and statesmen. And Dag's father was no exception. Hjalmar Hammarskjold had served as an official of the Swedish government in various capacities since he was a youth. Trained in the law, he had already won a reputation as one of the country's experts on international law by the time Dag was born.

A slender, handsome man, he was married in 1890 to attractive, dark-haired Agnes Almquist who came from an intellectual family of teachers, poets and philosophers. Agnes gave birth to four sons: Bo, Ake, Sten and Dag. Dag, the baby of the family, was fourteen years younger than Bo and ten years younger than Ake. Because Sten was only five years older, Dag felt closer to him than to the others.

Sweden in 1905—the year Dag was born—was a nation undergoing vast social and political changes. Under the reign of Oscar II, there had been growing industrialization and the passage of extensive social welfare legislation. Socially and economically, it was one of the most advanced nations in the world. But in politics, Sweden was experiencing a crisis.

For ninety years neighboring Norway had been united with Sweden, but disputes constantly arose between the two countries, so in 1905 the Norwegian Storting, or parliament, passed a dissolution act to scrap the union. This brought on a storm of controversy in Sweden which had to decide whether Norway would be allowed to depart in peace or whether to declare war. Many ultrapatriotic Swedes demanded that force be used to keep Norway in the union, but others, like Hjalmar Hammarskjold, were convinced it was wrong to withhold independence from a nation that desired it. In the end, King Oscar decided that a peaceful solution must be found. For this task he appointed a committee of four to go to Karlstad in central Sweden to meet with Norwegian representatives. Although Hjalmar Hammarskjold was then serving as the Minister of Culture, he was chosen to be one of the delegates.

Because of the urgency of the mission, little Dag's christening, scheduled to take place in early September, had to be delayed. On September 23, 1905, an agreement was signed in Karlstad which gave Norway her freedom. The happy news that there was to be no war was greeted with tears of joy by Swedes and Norwegians alike. When Hjalmar Hammarskjold returned from the successful meeting he told his wife, "I'm sorry the christening had to be put off, but it was done in the interests of peace. When he gets older, I'm sure our new son will understand."

The christening finally took place in late autumn in the ancient, spired Lutheran church in Jönköping. Among the presents was a beautiful silver cup sent by the negotiators who had participated with Hjalmar Hammarskjold in the conference at Karlstad. The gift was inscribed: "For the one too long without a name." In later years Dag's first "contribution" to the cause of peace became an oft-repeated family anecdote.

In 1907, when Dag was two, his father was appointed by the King to become Governor of Uppland, one of the largest and most important counties of Sweden. It was a great honor, and even though little Dag was too young to understand, he may have sensed that something important was in the wind when the family moved to the beautiful old city of Uppsala, county seat of Uppland, forty-five miles north of Stockholm. Here, in the historic old Governor's palace known as Vasa Castle, he was to spend his growing-up years. From the ornate halls of the great structure one could stare out at the twin spires of the beautiful Uppsala Cathedral where the coronation and burial of Swedish kings once took place. The cathedral stood tall and majestic in the cold northern light, and beyond it were the Gothic buildings of the ancient University of Uppsala, Sweden's leading institution of higher learning.

For a youngster like Dag, Uppsala, which prided itself on being a leading center of culture and boasted one of the finest libraries and museums in Europe, was a perfect place to spend a childhood. Even before he was out of elementary school he loved to visit the university grounds and stroll through the three-hundred-year-old buildings, staring with envy at the students as they hurried to their lectures carrying their heavy loads of books.

It was with his mother that young Dag felt the closest bond in his early years. There were few children his age to play with, and even his brother Sten, five years his senior, had more mature interests. Therefore out of sheer necessity he turned to his mother for the companionship he could not find elsewhere.

Agnes Hammarskjold gave her youngest son the love and attention he demanded as the baby of the family who needed her more than the others. She lavished on Dag a special care and concern her older sons did not seem to require or ask for. Mrs. Hammarskjold was a brilliant, cultured woman who had inherited the intellect and broad interests one expected in a family that boasted college professors, writers and artists. Her uncle, Carl Jonas Love Almquist, had been one of the giants of nineteenth-century literature and poetry in Sweden. She herself was interested in everything—music, poetry, art, literature, history and politics—and she did her best to transmit this feeling for culture and knowledge to all her sons, but particularly to Dag. For he, of all the Hammarskjold children, seemed to have an inclination for scholarship.

Like his brothers, Dag attended primary school in Uppsala, and while he soon earned a reputation as one of the most brilliant children in the school, it was at home that his real education took place. With her husband constantly occupied with important affairs of government, Mrs. Hammarskjold had a good deal of time on her hands, and she spent most of it with her children. There were servants, of course, and while many women would have been happy to put the care of their youngsters in the hands of maids and governesses, she accepted the responsibility for the intellectual development of her sons as a personal challenge.

Vasa Castle had a fine library, and under his mother's tutelage Dag read all the children's books available. One day he decided he would become a teacher. He confided his ambition to his mother, fearing that she would discourage him by pointing out that it was hardly a worthy goal for the son of one of Sweden's leading officials. To his surprise, she put her arms around him and declared, "If that is what you want to do most of all, you must do it. The profession of teaching is vital, for the teacher molds the future."

In spite of his brilliance at school, which might have caused resentment and envy, Dag soon won the respect of his schoolmates. For one thing, he had the pseudo maturity that children develop when they spend much of their time with adults—and this had an awing effect on the others at school. Moreover, despite his slender physique, the blond-haired, blue-eyed youngster had a great deal of stamina, and on the rare occasions when he had to fight he managed to hold his own through speed and physical endurance rather than with muscle or skill. His brother Sten liked to boast after a school fracas that "Dag may read books but he's no softie."

After one or two fights his classmates learned to leave him alone. For his part, Dag did not enjoy even the sight of physical violence, and once he succeeded in winning the respect of the other youngsters he often stepped in and patched up their quarrels. Since he had few intimate friends and preferred reading a book to taking sides in schoolboy feuds, his apparent aloofness proved to be an advantage in his role of elementary school peacemaker. This lesson, learned before he was ten, was never forgotten.

The year 1914 saw two events that changed Dag's mind about becoming a teacher. In February his father was named by the King to serve as Prime Minister of Sweden, thus becoming the most important man in the kingdom, next to the King himself. Then, barely five months later, on June 28, a Serbian youth named Gavrilo Princip assassinated Archduke Francis Ferdinand, heir to the Austro-Hungarian throne, and set off World War I.

The pre-1914 world of Dag's childhood had been a relatively stable one. True, there had been international intrigues marked by shifting alliances and political controversy throughout Europe, and barely a year had gone by without a revolution or "small war" taking place in some corner of the globe. Yet these conflicts had been local in scope and limited to a few countries, and for the most part the delicate scales on which international peace rested remained in precarious balance. For the first decade and a half of the twentieth century, therefore, life in much of the world had been blessed by a momentary freedom from the threat of war.

Particularly in Sweden were the people untouched by the hatreds and fears and passions that had written bloody chapters in recent history. Sweden had not been involved in a war for more than a century, and for the Swedish people peace had been transmuted into a way of life. War as a means of settling international disputes had become for most Swedes an unthinkable solution. Moreover, the atmosphere of national tranquillity was enhanced by social and economic progress that had given Sweden one of the highest standards of living in the world and by a form of government which, in spite of the presence of a king, was a democracy that guaranteed the people a degree of political freedom enjoyed in few other nations.

Once World War I began, Sweden, true to its century-old tradition, sought to stay out of the hostilities. Under the leadership of Prime Minister Hammarskjold, declarations were issued setting forth the government's refusal to take sides and insisting on the observance of Sweden's neutral rights by the warring nations. But the nature of world wars is such that its tragic effects are invariably felt by neutrals as well as by the combatants themselves. In Sweden the impact of the conflict was felt deeply. Some three hundred Swedish merchant ships were sunk by mines or in attacks by German and Allied submarines. Notes of protest were sent by the government to the opponents but the losses continued. In addition, both sides enforced blockades that further restricted trade. A shortage of goods resulted, and rationing had to be introduced.

With life in Sweden directly affected, it was little wonder that the people were as interested in the war's progress as if their country were a participant. Newspapers carried lengthy daily accounts of the fighting and for many it was the main topic of conversation.

Adult tensions and concern with a war that had extended to within a few miles of Sweden's shores communicated itself to the children. Like youngsters everywhere, they were caught up in a frenzied preoccupation with martial matters. The constant talk of guns, soldiers and battlefield heroics seized their imagination. In Stockholm, Malmo, Uppsala and the other cities and towns of Sweden small boys raced up and down the sidewalks using kitchen saucepans for helmets and brandishing homemade wooden rifles in fierce attacks on an imaginary enemy.

At first ten-year-old Dag was not entirely immune to the martial fever that had gripped Sweden's youth. The picture in his mind's eye of long lines of Swedish soldiers in colorful uniforms marching in precise military formation to the sound of trumpets and the beat of drums stirred his emotions. His recollection of the weapons hanging in the castle at Jönköping and of the stories he had heard of earlier generations of Hammarskjolds who had fought to defend Sweden's honor in wars long past added to his patriotic fervor. Moreover, as the son of the Prime Minister he could not help but be even more aware than most youngsters of Sweden's difficulties as a neutral in a world engulfed by war.

As Prime Minister, Hjalmar Hammarskjold had to spend most of his time in Stockholm, but he and his family continued to reside in Uppsala, only forty-six miles away. Around the great dining table in Vasa Castle Dag heard much talk about the violation of Sweden's neutrality by Germany and the Allied nations. In his ten-year-old mind he was convinced that as the leading minister of the Swedish government his father had the power to declare war on the countries that were attacking Sweden's ships, and he was at a loss to understand why this was not done. Instead he heard his father speak of maintaining peace and "patient diplomacy." Almost shamefaced, he found it hard to reconcile such talk with the stories of Swedish triumphs in battle in his schoolbooks and the legends of brave Viking forebears who had ruled the seas and struck terror in the hearts of the enemy.

With a precise logic Dag recalled his own early fights at school and how, in spite of his distaste of physical violence, he had accepted the challenges of the other boys. He had fought in order not to be considered a coward, for some instinctive sense had told him then that a refusal to respond to their taunts and jibes would have meant being at their mercy forever. Wasn't it true of nations as well as of people? he asked himself.

The perplexing question troubled him for many weeks until one evening he blurted out his feelings to his father. Wouldn't the rest of the world consider Sweden a cowardly nation if she did not fight when her ships were sunk? he demanded.

Hjalmar Hammarskjold stared up at his youngest son thoughtfully from behind the huge desk that had been in the family for generations, and put down the reports he had been

studying. Yes, it was quite true that no nation, if it were to retain its self-respect and the respect of its fellow nations, could
afford to be considered a coward, he explained patiently. But it
was equally true that other countries did not think of Sweden as
a cowardly nation. In war, thousands of innocent men, women
and children lose their lives, he added, and for this reason governments should not declare war lightly. Swedish ships were
being sunk, and that was a tragedy; but it was an outgrowth of
a world-wide tragedy—an accident that happened when nations
went to war—and not the result of purposeful design by either
side in the fighting.

For this reason, Hjalmar Hammarskjold told his son, it was
his job as Prime Minister to see to it that Sweden remained at
peace so that the hundreds of deaths that had already resulted
from the accidental sinking of Swedish ships would not grow
into the thousands of deaths that would be the inevitable result
if Sweden were to declare war against either side.

He paused, then concluded solemnly that the real answer was
for Sweden and all the other nations to join together in an effort
to eliminate war altogether, for if the present conflict proved
anything it demonstrated that once fighting started all nations
suffer, neutrals as well as those who actually fought in the war.

During the next days and weeks Dag thought a great deal
about the words his father had spoken and decided they were
wise words. It was then that he gave up his earlier ambition to
become a teacher and made up his mind to become a statesman
like his father.

Chapter Three

STUDENT DAYS

In March of 1917 Hjalmar Hammarskjold gave up his post as Prime Minister of Sweden.

For three years he had performed the arduous task of charting a neutral course in stormy international seas. He had hoped to keep his nation off the shoals of war, and in this he had succeeded. Now, with the danger of involvement in the conflict eliminated, he decided to return to his permanent post as Governor of Uppland. A basic reason was his desire to spend more time with his family, whom affairs of state had forced him to neglect in the past.

Dag, too, was growing older, and with age came a keener understanding of his father's beliefs and ideals. Out of this appreciation grew a stronger bond of love and respect between father and son. While Dag's relationship with his mother was still close, he began to see his father in a heroic light he had never recognized before.

On January 10, 1920, the League of Nations was established. It was the first major organization of countries ever created for the preservation of peace and international cooperation. Since it was the culmination of ideas and plans for international organization dating from the seventeenth century, for idealistic young Dag Hammarskjold, who was not yet fifteen, it was a thrilling moment in history. Sweden, of course, was one of the first nations to join the League, and Hjalmar Hammarskjold, as one of Sweden's leading experts on international law, was frequently called in by the government for consultation.

Dag, who avidly followed the progress of the new world organization in the newspapers, loved to debate with his father about the future of the League. He was surprised and dismayed that his unalloyed optimism was not shared by the older Hammarskjold.

His father had been a Swedish member of the Hague International Board of Arbitration since 1904, and in 1907 he had served as Sweden's leading delegate to the Hague Peace Conference. With the wisdom of long experience in international relations, he recognized some of the shortcomings of the League. For example, it had been a great disappointment to him that the United States, one of the most powerful nations in the world, had refused to join. Yet he did not want to destroy his youngest son's enthusiasm, so he explained patiently that the existence of an organization dedicated to peace did not guarantee peace. "The real test," he pointed out, "is the willingness of the member states to see that the concept of international law and order is enforced. Only the future holds that answer."

Meanwhile Dag, now in secondary school, continued to establish a brilliant academic record. He devoured books in almost every subject and had a facility for remembering everything he read. Because of this gift of glancing through something once and knowing it perfectly, he rarely had to prepare for exams. Even his father could not hide his pride at his son's intellectual capacity. "You know, if I had Dag's brains," said the man who had been Prime Minister of Sweden to a visitor, "I could have gone far."

In spite of the apparent ease with which he mastered his studies, Dag was a hard worker. He was not content to stop at the assignments given by his teachers but struck out on his own, reading advanced works of literature, history and political science. For recreation he read books about music and art.

In 1923, when he was eighteen, he graduated from secondary school with honors and enrolled at the University of Uppsala for a bachelor of arts degree. The university, which his father had attended and served as a member of the law faculty in 1891, was the oldest and most important of Swedish institutions of higher learning. State controlled and coeducational, it had been founded in 1477. The university library, with more than one million volumes and nineteen thousand manuscripts, housed some of the most valuable original documents in the world.

For Dag, who at eight had walked through the university halls awed by the atmosphere of scholarship that seemed to permeate every brick and stone, it was a proud moment.

On the advice of his parents he chose French, history of literature and practical philosophy as his majors. "The broader your background," said his father, "the broader your outlook, no matter what you choose to do in later life. That is why an education in the liberal arts is valuable."

In attending the University of Uppsala, Dag was following a well-established family tradition. Not only had his father gone there, but so had his older brothers, Bo, Ake and Sten. Bo was already making his mark as a government expert in social welfare legislation, and Ake, a lawyer, seemed destined for a distinguished career in jurisprudence. Sten, with artistic and literary talents, had gone to the United States to do postgraduate work at the Columbia University School of Journalism in New York City.

The habit of working hard that Dag had developed in elementary and secondary school was an advantage at Uppsala. The university professors were not like his earlier teachers who kept after their pupils on a day-by-day basis to get them to do homework assignments. Many of the Uppsala faculty were distinguished scholars who expected their students to accept the responsibilities of young adults. They made it clear at the outset that they were not there to spoon-feed their classes. Required assignments would be few and far between. If the students were to derive benefit from higher education they must do a great deal of studying on their own.

For many of the lazier students who had been used to doing just what was assigned to them and little more, the transition from secondary school to the university was a difficult one. At the end of the first semester a great many were forced to drop out because of failing grades. Dag, however, thrived on this educational regimen. He loved to study, and he especially enjoyed the freedom to do additional work on his own. The ability to glance through something once—and know it—amazed his professors just as it had confounded his parents and his secondary school teachers. At the end of the year he was on the university honor rolls for academic achievement.

Some of the more socially-minded students looked at Dag askance. They could not understand his preference for hard work and his single-minded devotion to study. He shied away from the various social activities that characterized life in a university town. He did not care for dancing and refused to get involved with girls. On Wednesday and Saturday evenings, when the others were out dancing, Dag studied. And he was rarely seen in the beer halls that served as the focal point of social activities for the many members of the student body.

In part, his preference for being alone was due to an iron sense of self-discipline. He feared that social activities would distract him from his real purpose—the acquisition of an education —and he had made up his mind at the outset not to allow anything to interfere with his studies.

But there was another reason, too, a reason of which perhaps he himself was not entirely aware. It was an innate shyness that made him ill at ease with other young people. Since early childhood he had had few friends his own age. Most of his time had been spent with adults—his parents and their guests, including leading government officials and foreign diplomats. As a result, he had somehow failed to develop the easy relationship with his contemporaries that his fellow students displayed. His intellectual interests were more advanced than theirs, and he couldn't help feeling that their youthful preoccupation with dancing and girls was something of a waste of time.

With adults, on the other hand, he could converse in articulate fashion and feel perfectly at ease. Between classes he preferred to spend an hour debating with his philosophy or literature professor over a cup of hot chocolate to arguing about the attractiveness of various girl students over a stein of foaming ale. For this reason many of his classmates considered him reserved and unfriendly, even aloof.

The few friendships he did make came about because of his love for skiing. Like skating and skiing, winter sports were a way of life in Sweden, and Dag had developed an interest in skiing ever since the winter holidays he had spent as a child at Jönköping. On weekends when fresh snow blanketed the ground, Dag and a few companions would take down their skis and board a train to one of the many winter resorts that abounded within a few hours' ride from Uppsala.

Dag was an enthusiastic, if not a particularly good, skier; his gifts were power and endurance rather than grace. Recognizing his own limitations, he did not try to copy the fancy maneuvers or dangerous jumps of the experts. "Frankly, you're better at getting up the mountainside than down," a puffing companion —one of the university's best skiers—quipped one day while trying unsuccessfully to keep up with Dag as they climbed the ski trail back to the top of the hill.

At night, around a crackling log fire, the students sipped hot drinks and discussed ways of improving their technique. Here, Dag was in his element, for he had read a great deal more about the art of skiing than any of the others, and while he did not have the coordination or muscular control of the born skier, he *had* mastered the theory. When he talked his companions listened with respect, for they were constantly awed by his vast store of knowledge.

Dag was also intrigued by mountain climbing. While there wasn't the time to indulge this hobby to the same extent as skiing, he often visited some of the nearby mountains—steep hills really—to improve his technique and toughen his leg muscles.

In the warmer months there were other sports, like swimming, boating and tennis, to help him relax after long hours of constant study.

But aside from sports, most of his hobbies were cultural in

nature. He enjoyed attending concerts and art exhibits, and sometimes, when he was tired, he would simply wind up the Gramophone, put a record on the turntable and close his eyes and listen for an hour or two to the magic notes as they poured out of the machine. His favorite composers were Johann Sebastian Bach and Antonio Vivaldi, the seventeenth-century violinist and composer who wrote operas, choral cantatas and violin concertos. There was an orderliness about their music that relaxed his mind and brought a curious sense of peace.

In addition to reading for his courses, Dag continued to read for pleasure as well. His tastes ranged from classical writers like Goethe and Cervantes to contemporary novelists, but he also haunted the university library for books on botany, zoology, geography and a host of other subjects. Moreover, even though he had become fluent in French, German and English at school, he was not satisfied and began to teach himself classical Greek.

His studies in philosophy and history gave him a familiarity with the great thinkers and heroic figures of the past. One of the stories that fascinated him was that of Thomas à Becket, the enigmatic twelfth-century English prelate who rose to become Chancellor of England under Henry II. In this role Becket served as a trusted royal adviser and military leader.

In order to control the Church, which had been opposing him, Henry appointed Becket Archbishop of Canterbury. Then a strange thing happened. Instead of remaining subservient to the King's orders, Becket adopted a life of great austerity and consecrated himself solely to the needs of the Church and the glory of God. He became a "God-intoxicated" man, dedicated to fulfilling his role as head of the Church in conscientious fashion.

Becket antagonized the King by opposing him when he felt the King's actions were against the best interests of the Church, even though he knew he was risking his life in doing so. Murdered in Canterbury Cathedral in 1170 by knights loyal to the King, he was made a saint three years later.

To Dag, the story of Thomas à Becket was a haunting and

beautiful one. But it raised a disturbing philosophical question: How could a man's basic loyalties change so radically? Becket's secular allegiance to Henry II had changed overnight to a spiritual loyalty to the Church and God. What was there about the nature of faith and idealism that could make a man forget his own selfish interests and rigid, conventional loyalties and raise him to the heroic proportions of a saint? It was an intriguing question, Dag told himself, one that men had undoubtedly been asking themselves since the beginning of recorded history.

In 1925, two years later after he had entered the university, Dag received the baccalaureate degree. He told the officials of the institution that he wanted to continue his studies and specialize in economics. In choosing economics he was heeding the advice of his father. He had declared his intention of becoming a lawyer, but his father had pointed out that a true understanding of the law could come only from a knowledge and understanding of the various forces that shape man's existence at a particular time in history. The real lawmakers, Hjalmar Hammarskjold told him, were not the lawyers or judges but the scientists and inventors who transformed society and thus forced changes in the laws that would reflect society's changing needs. "A lawyer must first of all be a student of political economy," he said.

For the next three years Dag specialized in economics, with the understanding that he would go on to his law studies afterward. In 1928 he was awarded a licentiate of philosophy degree in economics. Again he was among the top honor winners in his class, and he was accepted immediately by the law faculty as a matriculant for a bachelor of laws.

Although preoccupied with his studies, he continued to maintain a close interest in international events which were now taking a fascinating turn. In many nations of the world, pacifist movements were making headway. Spurred on by the peace treaties of 1919 which greatly reduced the armaments of Germany and Austria, the proponents of a general reduction in armaments agitated continuously. The League of Nations assumed a leading role in this campaign, and a conference in Washington, D.C., in 1921 had resulted in an agreement whereby Great Britain, France, Japan, Italy and the United States—although it was not a member of the League of Nations—had agreed to limit naval armaments. Now, as the decade was coming to a close, there was talk of holding another conference to secure even more drastic limitations.

Dag, of course, was enthusiastic about these developments. With an "I told you so" air, he asserted that his father's early pessimism about the effectiveness of the League of Nations was proving to be groundless. The limitation of arms agreements certainly indicated a general desire to do away with war, he argued. But Hjalmar Hammarskjold retained his customary diplomat's caution. "I pray you are right," he told his son. "But the true test has not yet come. We will see it only when some nation chooses to build its military might regardless of world opinion. If the great nations of the world have the mutual desire and strength of purpose to back the League of Nations in action against the 'outlaw' nation, then indeed we may witness the beginnings of permanent peace in our lifetime."

Even his father's sober words were not enough to dampen Dag's idealism. He respected his father's knowledge and experience in most things, but in matters of this sort he couldn't help feeling that his father represented an outdated concept of conventional diplomacy. True, his father was a pacifist by temperament and conviction, but it was a theoretical pacifism that bore little relation to his role as a professional diplomat, Dag thought.

Almost self-righteously, he convinced himself that what was needed was a new generation of idealistic young diplomats who would eliminate the secrecy and suspicion from international relations, thus reducing resentments and tension. "Open covenants, openly arrived at," was the way Woodrow Wilson, the American president, had put it after the end of the great war. If this policy were followed, Dag believed, the efforts of the League of Nations would be strengthened.

In 1930, Dag received his diploma as a bachelor of law. But the world into which he stepped after leaving the Uppsala campus was radically different from what he had anticipated just a few months before—for Sweden and the other nations had suddenly found themselves plunged into a global economic depression.

Chapter Four

THE TROUBLED DECADE

The week after Dag completed his law studies at Uppsala his father made an important announcement. He was giving up the governorship of Uppland after twenty-three years! Dag received the news with mixed emotions. He had been only two when his father was appointed to the post by the King. For as long as he could remember the Governor's castle had been his home. Somehow, he could not imagine his parents living anywhere but in the great structure he had known all his life.

On the other hand, he realized that his father, at sixty-eight, was no longer young. Governing one of Sweden's largest provinces had not been easy. It had meant long hours, constant worry and a multitude of crises. He could recall the many times the elder Hammarskjold had driven himself to the point of physical exhaustion. Common sense told Dag that after forty-five years of service to Sweden, his father was entitled to a well-earned retirement.

In the summer of 1930, the family moved to Stockholm where Mrs. Hammarskjold found a spacious, comfortable apartment. Dag, still unmarried, agreed to stay with his parents. They had barely settled in Stockholm when Dag received a call from Bo. His brother, who had been working on a revised social welfare program for the government, told him about a post that was open as Secretary of the Royal Commission on Unemployment. It called for a young man with a good background in economics. Was Dag interested? Indeed he was, Dag replied immediately, and his brother agreed to submit his name.

A few days later he was called down and interviewed by members of the commission. Later that week he received word that he had gotten the job.

To Dag the post seemed to hold out an exciting challenge. The depression had caused unemployment and hardship, and even Sweden's social welfare programs could not cope with these problems. Clearly, additional machinery was needed; but before new programs could be worked out, careful studies had to be made. Because of this the Royal Commission on Unemployment suddenly had assumed great importance. With the jobless forming long lines at social welfare centers, the dimensions of the problem had to be established.

As Secretary of the commission, Dag immediately undertook a comprehensive study to find out the pattern of unemployment. It was a backbreaking task, for there was an enormous amount of research to be done and the commission's budget did not provide for adequate clerical assistance. Most of his time was spent in libraries and in various government offices collecting data that had never been compiled and examined before.

He also enrolled at the University of Stockholm for a doctor of philosophy degree. Because of his work with the commission, he decided it would be best to take it in the field of economics. For the subject of his doctoral thesis he chose to deal with the way unemployment and other dangerous trends could spread like an epidemic throughout the economy, if not treated promptly and vigorously. The university officials approved his outline.

In spite of his heavy burden of work and study, Dag managed to find time for other interests. He continued to ski in the winter, and on weekends when it did not snow there were long hikes in the countryside. In the summer he liked to take extended bicycle trips, stopping off at little inns along the way.

Now that he was earning his own living, Dag could easily have taken an apartment of his own, but he chose to stay with his parents for his mother's sake. Two of his brothers were out of the country—Ake was a registrar at the International Court of Justice at The Hague and Sten was still in the United States

working for *The New York Times*—and Dag knew how much
his presence meant to her. Indeed, for Agnes Hammarskjold,
her youngest son was still the focal point of her existence. Every
day on his way home for lunch Dag would stop off and buy her
a bunch of flowers which she greeted with delight and placed in
a vase as a centerpiece for the dining table. And in the evenings,
he discussed his work with his mother and father much as he
had done when he was a schoolboy.

His mother showed a single-minded concern for his welfare
and comfort, sometimes forgetting that he was twenty-five years
old. Before he left on an outing she reminded him to dress
warmly, and hardly a week passed that she did not plead with
him to stop working so hard.

In spite of her remonstrations, Dag attacked his work with a
furious, driving energy that impressed his superiors. They liked
his clear-thinking approach to economic problems and saw in
his preliminary studies of unemployment trends a valuable
guide for future planning. His doctoral work at the University
of Stockholm was also taking impressive shape, and one of his
professors indicated that if the final thesis measured up to the
promise of the early draft there was a possibility that he might
even be offered a post on the faculty.

Nevertheless, what might have been a busy, satisfying existence was shadowed by the cloud of national despair that seemed
to hang over the land. Everywhere people were out of work, and
the newspapers were full of gloomy reports about the future of
the economy. Sensitive and introspective, Dag could not help
but be affected by the knowledge that throughout Sweden men,
women and children were suffering economic privation. Sometimes the awareness of his own good fortune gave him a nagging
sense of guilt.

He was also depressed by the sad state of world affairs. What
just a few short years before had seemed like a trend toward
greater international stability and peace now took a drastic turn
in the other direction.

In June of 1931, Japan seized Manchuria from China and

turned it into a puppet Japanese state. The Japanese had eyed Manchuria hungrily for a long time, and now with a weak Chinese government in power they felt the time had come to strike. The Chinese protested. The League of Nations issued a condemnation of Japan's Manchurian policy and asked that her troops be withdrawn. The Japanese refused. To the dismay of people throughout the world the League of Nations took no further action, and Japan remained in control of Manchuria.

The following February, a General Conference for the Limitation of Armaments was held in Geneva, Switzerland, under the auspices of the League. Its purpose was to broaden the disarmament agreements of the previous decade. The conference ended in failure.

A few months later, in April of 1932, elections in Germany evidenced strong support for a new ultranationalist political group known as the National Socialist or Nazi party. It was headed by a funny-looking mustached Austrian named Adolf Hitler. Hitler's platform was a strange and frightening admixture of German racial supremacy concepts, anti-Semitism and a promise to rebuild Germany's military might. Early the following year, Hitler was named dictator of Germany, and Germany withdrew from the League of Nations.

This series of tragic international events, coming within the short space of two years, gave Dag a sense of futility. Fortunately, his mental state was buoyed somewhat by the satisfaction of learning that his doctoral thesis had been accepted. Entitled "Expansion of Market Trends," it was acclaimed as a brilliant piece of work by members of the faculty. In June of 1933 he was awarded his doctor of philosophy degree and offered a position as Assistant Professor of Political Economy at the University of Stockholm. He accepted and began teaching on a limited schedule so that he could retain his job with the Royal Commission.

Word of Dag's incisive study of economic trends did not stop at the university gates. The findings in his doctoral thesis and the results of his brilliant studies for the Royal Commission on

Unemployment came to the attention of officials of the Swedish Finance Ministry. One morning he received an invitation to visit the ministry. Surprised but curious, he showed up at the appointed time and was told that he had just been named Secretary of the National Bank of Sweden, the most important financial institution in the land! Excited by this wholly unexpected news, he rushed home to tell his parents.

Dag worked hard to master the intricate financial and economic details involved in administering an official government bank. It was not an easy task, for there was a prodigious amount to be learned. Every day his desk was swamped with reports on industrial, business and monetary policies. Here again his astuteness in understanding and evaluating complicated reports and his photographic memory for details paid off. He soon gained a reputation among the Board of Governors of the bank as the man to be called in for tightly analyzed reports of intricate economic problems.

Early in 1936 the government press office released an official announcement that Dag Hammarskjold had been named Undersecretary of the Ministry of Finance of Sweden. The news was published extensively in the Swedish press which also pointed out that at thirty-one he was the youngest man ever named to that post.

Dag's amazingly swift rise delighted his mother but frightened him. As Undersecretary he was now in a position of national prominence. Suddenly he began to receive telephone calls from newspaper reporters and others who requested his comments on a host of matters ranging from economic problems to foreign affairs. He was asked to write articles for magazines, and a few publishers offered him flattering sums of money to write books on how to solve the nation's economic woes.

Startled by this rash of personal publicity which made him uncomfortable, he turned to his father for advice. That experienced veteran of public life smiled wryly and told him that he must learn to live with his new prominence. "A government official exists in a goldfish bowl," Hjalmar Hammarskjold told his son. "It makes life difficult but it is unavoidable. You must develop a thick skin against criticism *and* flattery and do your work with an eye only to what is in the best interest of Sweden and her people."

Dag took this sound advice and adopted a firm policy of saying no to requests for personal interviews and statements. He was polite but firm. After a few weeks the newspapers decided that when the youthful new Undersecretary replied "no comment" to a question, he meant it. Instead of resenting what they at first had supposed to be an aloofness toward the press, they began to respect him for his determination to retain his anonymity.

With his new post Dag inherited important new responsibilities. He quickly enhanced his reputation among government officials as a master of financial and economic details. The special assignments handed him included drawing up plans for improving Sweden's foreign trade position, procuring raw materials and stabilizing the country's economic and wage control programs. In the field of economics Dag was an exponent of the ideas of the famous English economist John Maynard Keynes, who believed that the state had a basic responsibility for controlling business fluctuations and preventing unemployment. At Uppsala he had studied Keynes's theories carefully, although in the 1920's they had not yet gained the prominence they were to achieve after the beginning of the depression. Now, this background in Keynesian economics paid off, for many of the older financial authorities were relatively unfamiliar with Keynes's ideas and had to turn to Dag to learn about them. In a short time the young Undersecretary of Finance became known as a leading authority in the application of these new theories to Sweden's economy.

Although his duties did not include responsibility in the area of foreign affairs, he soon found that economic planning for the nation could not be divorced from its foreign policy. Many of his activities brought him in close contact with the Foreign Office, particularly when he was working with foreign trade problems. He read the foreign reports religiously and followed international developments in the press on a day-by-day basis.

Unfortunately, the news from abroad continued to be disturbing. By 1935 anti-Jewish riots were being organized in Germany by the Nazi government and compulsory military service was reintroduced by Hitler in direct violation of the Treaty of Versailles. To counter the German threat a mutual assistance pact was signed between Czechoslovakia and Russia. Later France joined the alliance.

But most disheartening of all was the invasion of the African kingdom of Abyssinia by Fascist Italy which was headed by Benito Mussolini. The League of Nations Assembly met on October 9, 1935 and called for the enforcement of sanctions against Italy. Undeterred by the League's verbal condemnation of its actions, Italy continued to pour in troops and planes to fight the ill-equipped Abyssinians. By the following February, a native army of eighty thousand men armed mostly with spears and swords was decimated, and three months later Mussolini announced the annexation of Abyssinia. Haile Selassie, King of Abyssinia, fled from Addis Ababa, the capital, and appeared before the League of Nations to plead for the continuance of sanctions against Italy and the recognition of Abyssinia's claim to independence.

During those hectic days when the whole world waited tensely to see what the League would do, Dag sat at home with his parents every evening glued to the radio to learn the latest developments. Would the big nations take action against the aggressor or would they turn a deaf ear to little Abyssinia's cause? This was the real test he had spoken of, Hjalmar Hammarskjold told Dag solemnly. It was a clear-cut issue, he pointed out, of whether the world wanted international law and order or whether the League of Nations was doomed to failure.

By June 30 the verdict was in. The League voted to reject Haile Selassie's plea and refused to take effective action against Italy.

Tears welled in Hjalmar Hammarskjold's eyes on that warm

summer evening as he informed his son that the League had failed the supreme test. With its peace-enforcing machinery a failure, he declared in a voice that quivered with emotion, the League had demonstrated to potential aggressors that they could attack other nations with impunity.

Dag sat and listened and nodded despondently. For the first time he admitted to himself that his father had been right all along. Now he saw clearly what he had refused to see before—that the mere existence of an international organization did not of itself guarantee peace; not unless it was backed by member nations armed with the will and moral courage to enforce a basic concept of world law and order.

Like millions of idealistic men and women all over the world, Dag recognized in the failure of the League of Nations the betrayal of his own hopes and dreams for a better world. The lack of determination of the great powers to carry out their obligations as members of the international organization was an indication of moral cowardice, he felt. In a curious way, he told himself bitterly, even the United States, which had refused to join the League in the first place, had displayed more forthrightness than the member nations. The American people and their leaders had been unwilling to shoulder the responsibilities of League membership and had made their attitude clear by refusing to join it. They had been shortsighted and unrealistic perhaps, but at least they were honest from the first about their intentions. The leaders of the nations that *had* joined the League, however, were guilty of something far worse—inspiring in mankind the dream of peace, then dashing that dream to the ground.

But the bright hopes for an orderly world that had begun to tarnish with the Japanese invasion of Manchuria and had been broken with the League's failure to act against Italy, were to receive additional blows. In 1936 a bloody civil war broke out in Spain with Fascist forces led by General Francisco Franco seeking to overthrow a legally elected Republican government. Almost immediately men and materials were poured into Spain, with Communist Russia helping the Loyalists and Fascist Italy

and Nazi Germany assisting Franco's forces. The enfeebled
League of Nations pleaded that there be no foreign intervention
in the civil war, but the request was contemptuously ignored.
The fighting went on with outside assistance continuing to flow
in to both sides. Within a year, Franco was able to proclaim
himself dictator of Spain.

At the same time, halfway across the world, Japanese armies
invaded China in full force, resuming where they had left off
six years before after taking Manchuria.

For the Hammarskjold family, 1937 was a year clouded with
personal tragedy as well. Dag and his parents received word
from the Netherlands that Ake, who was still serving with the
International Court of Justice at The Hague, had been taken
ill. Mr. and Mrs. Hammarskjold took the first train out of
Stockholm. When they arrived in the Netherlands they were
told that their son's condition was critical. The doctors diag-
nosed it as rheumatic fever. Less than a week later, Ake was
dead at the age of forty-two. When Dag met his grief-stricken
parents at the railroad station in Stockholm, they were accompanied by the casket containing the body of his older brother.
Dag, ordinarily so self-contained, wept openly at the funeral.

In March of 1938, Hitler precipitated a political crisis in
Austria by threatening an invasion, then sent his Nazi troops
into that country to annex it to Germany. His appetite whetted
by this easy success, he next threatened the government of
Czechoslovakia for allegedly encouraging the persecution of resi-
dents in the Sudeten area of Czechoslovakia who were of German extraction. The British and French tried to negotiate an
agreement that would appease the Germans, but Hitler continued to apply pressure on the Czech government. Finally,
Prime Minister Neville Chamberlain of Great Britain and
Premier Edouard Daladier of France met with Hitler and Mussolini in Munich, Germany. On September 21 Chamberlain and
Daladier agreed that Czechoslovakia would have to cede the
Sudeten area to Hitler in return for a Nazi promise to maintain

peace in Europe and respect the integrity of the remaining Czechoslovakian territory.

In Prague and the other cities of Czechoslovakia, the people listened in stunned silence to the news that their nation had been compromised by the British and French in a desperate attempt to buy "peace in our time," as Chamberlain phrased it upon his return to England.

With each day bringing headlines of a new international crisis and with nations trembling under threats of aggression by ruthless dictators, it seemed to Dag that the whole world was about to explode. He had the sickening feeling that mankind was plunging headlong into an abyss of mass destruction and could not help itself. He tried to escape his feelings of depression by burying himself in his work and in his books and by resuming the bicycling trips and mountain climbing he had given up after his elevation to the undersecretaryship.

The escape even took the form of expeditions to the untamed wilderness of Lapland. Here in the north of Scandinavia, above the Arctic Circle, he found a place of immense beauty, a region far removed from the passions and hatreds of civilization. With a friend, Gosta Lundquist, Dag traversed an ancient crystalline plateau in North Sweden, and continued pressing northward toward the treeless frozen tundra. They passed glacial lakes and marshes and paused to drink in the beauty of the rugged, picturesque coast with its deep, sculptured fiords. They stayed in Lapp settlements, and Dag fell in love with this amazing nomadic people.

The Laplanders were short and dark-haired, with spare muscular bodies and fantastic powers of physical endurance. Isolated from the rest of Europe, they had remained unchanged in their customs for centuries, traveling throughout the Scandinavian Peninsula with their huge herds of reindeer, on which they depended for food, clothing and shelter. In this serene, hospitable people Dag recognized an absence of the tension and fear that seemed to infect more advanced societies. Later he wrote of his admiration for the Laplanders and "their faithful adherence to a form of society and tradition with roots stretching far beyond historical time."

But the escape Dag sought could not be a permanent one, as he himself realized only too well. Each time he returned from a mountain climbing or bicycling trip or an expedition up north he was jolted back to the harsh realities of the moment. The newspapers and radio commentators all talked of the possibility of war in Europe and the confidential reports from the Swedish Foreign Office confirmed these frightening news announcements. Sometimes Dag imagined he could almost smell the acrid odor of gunpowder in the air.

Early in 1939 Germany seized Czechoslovakia in violation of the Munich agreement with which Great Britain and France had tried to appease Hitler. A few weeks later, the Nazi dictator made demands on Poland for the return of territories that Germany had lost in World War I.

All over Europe, now, troops were being called up and nerves were growing tenser all the time. On August 21, the news went out to the stunned democracies that Soviet Russia and Germany had signed a ten-year mutual nonaggression pact.

Ten days later, long lines of gray-uniformed Nazi troops goose-stepped across the border into Poland while German planes dived low over Warsaw, Cracow and other Polish cities, dropping tons of bombs on the civilian populations.

On September 3, 1939, British Prime Minister Chamberlain appeared before Parliament and announced that Hitler had ignored an ultimatum to get out of Poland. Consequently, he declared, a state of war existed between Germany and Great Britain.

World War II had begun.

Chapter Five

THE PROMISE OF PEACE

For Dag the outbreak of hostilities between the Allies and the Axis powers posed serious problems of personal conscience and principle. Like many of his countrymen, he was caught up in a conflict of divided ideals and emotions. Sweden had been committed to a course of peace and neutrality for well over a century, and by instinct the Swedish people held strong pacifist principles. By joining the League of Nations they had indicated their abhorrence of waging war except when necessary to maintain world order through an international body.

Because of the failure of the members of the League to take collective action the League had failed. Now war had broken out again, but it was a conflict waged, not in the name of an international organization of nations, but a war in the traditional pattern—between individual nation-states. If this were the only factor to be considered, the Swedish people undoubtedly would have been united in their desire to adhere to their traditional neutrality. But unfortunately the realities of life rarely allowed for a clear-cut choice.

Thus it was not a simple matter of deciding whether Sweden should declare war or maintain a strict neutrality. For while the conflict was between individual nations, many Swedes recognized it as a war for survival between peace-loving democracies on the one hand and the forces of ruthless barbarism on the other. Sweden was a highly cultured and civilized nation. Her people viewed the policies and actions of the Nazis and Fascists with loathing and disgust. Emotionally and intellectually, they

were on the side of the Allies, and many of them favored going
to war against the Axis powers in spite of their long history of
neutrality.

Dag himself was sickened by the stories of Nazi atrocities
against Jews and other minorities and considered Hitler a threat
to every civilized concept developed by man over a period of
two thousand years. Like many of his fellow officials in the government, however, he also knew that to declare war would be
an impractical gesture. Because of her geographical proximity
to Germany and her inadequate military and naval forces,
Sweden was in a strategically vulnerable position. In an all-out
war she would be conquered in a short time. Would it not be
better to remain officially neutral but to render assistance to the
Allies in more subtle ways?

These were the issues the Swedes were faced with in those
early months of World War II—difficult and complex issues
that called for the weighing of principle, tradition and strategy
on the delicate scales of governmental policy.

As Undersecretary of Finance, Dag was only incidentally
involved in the debates and endless discussions that went on
behind the closed doors of the Foreign Ministry. But he was
called upon to submit reports on international trade, the avail-
bility of natural resources and manufacturing output which were
needed to formulate a sound decision. As a result, Dag began
to realize, as perhaps he had never realized before, the tremendous responsibilities which his father had faced as Prime
Minister during World War I. Sometimes he smiled wryly as
he recalled his own former inability to understand the com-
plexities involved in making governmental decisions, especially
in foreign affairs. It had always seemed so easy—a simple matter of following one's ideals and doing the right thing. But
what was the right thing? Too often there was a world of difference between what should be done and what could be done,
Dag decided. It was evident most often during political cam-
paigns, when a politician sharply criticized an incumbent for
following certain policies only to discover, after being elected,

that knowledge of the full facts placed an entirely different complexion on problems.

In the end, Sweden decided on a policy of neutrality, just as it had in World War I. However, the government leaders were not at all certain in those early months of the war that such a course could be followed. They had no illusions about the brutal nature of naziism, and many, including Dag, half anticipated that Germany would invade Sweden. This fear was strengthened when Hitler's armies occupied neighboring Denmark and Norway. Sweden prepared to resist attack by calling up nearly eight hundred thousand troops. The Swedish people were realistic enough to understand that they could not prevent a German invasion; but they were determined to fight as hard as they could if such an attack did take place.

However, for some reason Hitler decided not to invade Sweden. Some experts felt that the magnificent underground resistance of the Danes and Norwegians had tied up so many German troops that the Nazis were convinced they could not spare the divisions needed to subdue the tough, well-trained Swedish army. Others concluded that Hitler felt the occupation of Sweden was not strategically necessary. But whatever the real reason, the Germans stayed out.

In spite of her declaration of official neutrality, Sweden quietly gave a great deal of assistance to the Allied cause. Through the Red Cross she harbored Danish and Norwegian refugees. Thousands of Jews were saved from extermination by fleeing to Swedish soil—from Denmark alone came five thousand Danish Jews who were smuggled into Sweden by the Danish underground when the German authorities ordered their arrest. Moreover Sweden permitted the creation of Danish and Norwegian "police forces" on her territory, many of whom made their way back to their native countries to join the underground.

Meanwhile, Soviet Russia, which had signed a pact with Hitler, proceeded to attack tiny Finland. Sweden now extended nonmilitary aid to Finland, just as she was doing for the opponents of Hitler. But it was a hopeless cause. In the battle of the pygmy against the giant, little Finland lost after five months of heroic resistance and was forced to sign a peace treaty with Russia that called for important territorial concessions.

For Dag the sorrow of observing the world at war twice in his own lifetime was given added dimension by another, more personal tragedy. Late in 1940, his mother died at the age of seventy-five. To the end, Agnes Hammarskjold had been one of the anchoring forces in her son's life. She had been a constant companion to him, and in his maturity he had leaned on her during times of crises, respecting her intelligence, charm and counsel.

Her death left him with a deep sense of loneliness and loss. Toward his father, who was now nearing seventy-nine, he felt a tender solicitude. His mother and father had been married for fifty years, and while Hjalmar Hammarskjold said little, Dag knew what his mother's passing must have meant to him.

For this reason he decided to stay on in the apartment with his father, even though the older man protested that he was well able to take care of himself and had plenty of work to keep him busy. Actually, while Hjalmar Hammarskjold was no longer active in government, he had long been a member of the Swedish Academy and chairman of its Nobel Institution. In this capacity he was responsible for examining the books of authors nominated for Nobel Prizes in Literature. The very apartment in which they lived was in a house owned by the Nobel Foundation. It overlooked a lovely tree-shaded park surrounding the Royal Library, and because of the delightful location Dag and his father decided not to move, in spite of the memories of Agnes Hammarskjold that were associated with it.

Once again his affinity for hard work stood Dag in good stead. By burying himself in his job more deeply than ever, he found a partial release from sorrow and loneliness following his mother's death. Moreover, because of the war there was plenty to do. Just as in 1914, Sweden, cut off from western Europe, found herself facing critical supply problems and inflationary pressures. As Undersecretary of the Ministry of Finance Dag was given the task of drafting price-control legislation and establishing other machinery to keep the economy running as smoothly and efficiently as possible under adverse circumstances.

In 1941 he was appointed Chairman of the Board of Governors of the Swedish National Bank while continuing to serve as Undersecretary of Finance.

One day he was called in by Ernst Wigforss, the Minister of Finance, and given a special assignment. "It will mean personal danger," the minister warned. "And it must remain top secret."

Dag listened intently as Wigforss described what he had in mind. Neighboring Norway, under the Nazi heel, had a large and active underground which was headed by a Norwegian ␣rnment-in-exile in England. To keep the underground fight-␣ ␣ied with arms and supplies required funds. The Swedish ␣t wanted to assist by extending economic credits to ␣ent-in-exile, but this required confidential negotia-␣e Nazis learned about it they would accuse Sweden ␣declaration of neutrality. Did Dag want to take ␣oung Undersecretary said yes.

␣ths he held conferences with Norwegian ␣ecret meeting places throughout Sweden. ␣gians were flown in at night from Eng-␣gled in from Norway under the eyes ␣d at the Norwegian-Swedish border. ␣oothly and Dag worked out agree-␣n government-in-exile with finan-␣nt as aid for wartime activities ␣conomic arrangements for the ␣not last forever," Wigforss ␣eaten we will have to help ␣result, Dag's assignment ␣for postwar economic

␣e Norwegian agents

were concluded, it was agreed that the final arrangements would have to have the approval of the top Norwegian leaders in England. At Wigforss' request, Dag agreed to fly to London to meet with the government-in-exile to conclude the agreements.

The plane assigned to Dag was one of a number of unmarked military transports used by the British for secret night operations. At regular intervals, the craft would fly to Sweden to pick up Allied air crews whose planes had been shot up by the Germans but who had managed to land in Sweden. The fliers would then be "interned" by the Swedish government until a transport came for them and flew them back to England while the Swedes "looked the other way."

On the evening that Dag was to fly to London, he was driven to an airport near Stockholm where he met the Norwegian representatives with whom he had been negotiating. They were issued inflatable life vests and parachutes and given instruction in their use. Then the party climbed aboard the huge transport and waited uneasily as the powerful motors roared to life.

It was just after dark when the plane soared into the heading almost due east. A heavy cloud cover offered protec from German fighters as they crossed the Skagerrak, the between Norway and Denmark. But when they broke ou the North Sea and turned southwest, the clouds thinn and here and there a star winked into view.

Dag had brought along a pocket edition of sixteenth French poems to while away the time on the long f while the other passengers dozed, he puffed on a cigar and read quietly by the dim cabin light.

Suddenly the plane began to veer sharply as if t gone crazy. The Norwegians awoke with a start fro pitching and looked at each other fearfully. A announced that they had been sighted by a fighter and that the transport was taking evasive

For the next few minutes the plane continu dive and bank from side to side while everyon Then the violent tossing ceased. The crew passengers that the pilot had flown into a cloud bank and succeeded in losing the Luftwaffe plane. The danger was over, he assured them. It was only then that one of the Norwegian diplomats who had been seated near Dag realized with a start that the Swedish Undersecretary had been reading unconcernedly throughout the excitement. "You must have nerves of steel, Mr. Hammarskjold," he said in amazement. "Why I practically forgot my own name."

Dag removed the cigar from his mouth and said wryly, "There's nothing like French poetry and a strong cigar to calm the nerves. Would you care to smoke one of mine?"

Upon his return to Stockholm after successfully completing the agreement with the Norwegian leaders in London, Dag and Finance Minister Wigforss worked out a program to provide similar financial credit to Denmark and Holland for postwar reconstruction.

For his services to Norway at the risk of his own safety, Dag was awarded the Grand Cross of the Order of St. Olav, a medal which the Norwegians bestowed very sparingly and only for contributions of major importance.

The United States and Russia were now in the war against Germany. As the offensive passed from the Axis powers to the Allied nations, the peoples of the free world dared to look forward once again to a time when the killing and bloodshed would cease.

In June of 1944 the Allies landed in Normandy to launch a massive invasion of Europe, while on the Russian plains the ragged, hard-pressed armies of the German "master race" began to retreat westward.

By the following spring it was plain that World War II was drawing to a close. Millions had died in the war; millions more were hungry, homeless and cold. Out of the death camps of Germany marched living skeletons to tell a story of barbarism unmatched in human history, a chilling tale of the butchery of millions of innocent men, women and children that was so fraught with horror and degradation as to defy the credibility of civilized people. These, then, were the victims of war and devastation and Nazi savagery who now constituted a living challenge to the conscience of mankind.

On April 25, 1945, an international conference was called in San Francisco, California. To it were invited all the countries in the world that were at war with Germany or Japan. These Allied nations were by now referred to as the "united nations," a name originated in 1942 by President Franklin D. Roosevelt. In addition, several other countries like Denmark, which had just been liberated, Argentina and several of the Soviet Socialist Republics were invited to participate. Each of these countries sent representatives to San Francisco.

The goal of the delegates was to fashion an organization to deal with the quarrels between nations that might lead to war, and provide for collective security against countries guilty of acts of aggression. The diplomats who attended the conference were deeply conscious of the fact that the people of the whole world longed for a lasting peace. They recognized, too, that all over the world, wherever people lived under foreign or domestic oppression, there was a growing demand for freedom and justice. So in their deliberations they gave special attention to the interests of the people as well as to the nations. It was stated at the conference that one of the purposes of the projected organization was to achieve international cooperation in "promoting and encouraging respect for human rights and for fundamental freedoms for all without distinction as to race, sex, language or religion."

The deliberations at the meeting lasted for weeks and included a great deal of wrangling about voting procedures and other important issues. But in the end, out of this great debate came a charter for an international body dedicated to the cause of peace. The delegates of fifty nations affixed their signatures to the document.

The date was June 26, 1945.

It was the day the United Nations Organization was born.

Chapter Six

PARIS INTERLUDE

Dag followed the events in San Francisco with deep interest. In spite of the disillusioning failure of the League of Nations, there was in him still a lingering spark of the enthusiasm that had kindled his youthful dreams of a world free of war. The naïve idealism of his teens and early twenties had given way to the hardheaded realism of maturity. At forty he understood what his father had tried to explain unsuccessfully when he was sixteen—that there was no simple road to peace.

Dag's interest in the United Nations was keen for another reason, too. His work in negotiating economic agreements with other nations had involved him more deeply than before in foreign affairs. Although he was still Undersecretary of the Ministry of Finance, his responsibilities cut across economic lines and touched the sensitive area of international diplomacy as well.

Early in 1945 the government decided to give him a post independent of the Finance Ministry; Minister Wigforss concurred in this decision. Dag was named Adviser on Economic and Financial problems to the Swedish Cabinet, and in this capacity he was free to take on jobs that did not fall within the confines of his former department.

While his title was that of "adviser," he was actually a "trouble shooter" for the Cabinet. Most of his assignments were in the "top priority" category—tasks that required the utmost skill.

In addition, Dag, who had already proven his ability as an economic analyst and coordinator, was given the job of organizing and coordinating all government planning on postwar economic problems. He studied the reports of the Ministries of Finance and Foreign Affairs and interrelated them in concise fashion for the Cabinet.

Because of his experience in arranging economic agreements with foreign governments, his duties also included foreign trade negotiations. He was instrumental, for example, in renegotiating trade agreements with Great Britain and the United States.

As a political economist, Dag recognized the role that economic interdependence plays in strengthening diplomatic relations between countries. For this reason he saw the United Nations as a world organization that would serve not only as a political forum but as an aid in promoting international economic cooperation, too. He studied the charter and organization of the United Nations carefully, in an effort to familiarize himself with all their intricacies.

Like Hammarskjold, the founders of the UN had seen clearly the relationship between politics and economics and had set up specialized agencies to study and coordinate international activities in the economic and social field and provide assistance for nations in need of help.

In the late summer of 1945, an event took place that altered the course of international relations for all time to come.

The hostilities in Europe had ended in May with the surrender of Germany. For the next three months the war against Japan continued to be fought in the Far East. Then, on August 6, an American B-29 bomber flew over the city of Hiroshima, Japan, and dropped a single bomb that pulverized sixty per cent of the city and left seventy-five thousand people dead and many more thousands wounded. The great mushroom cloud that boiled over Japan in the wake of the plane symbolized the beginning of a new and terrifying era in human history—the Atomic Age.

For the first time mankind was faced with the specter of man-created death and devastation on a mass scale capable of destroying civilization itself. Thus a revolutionary new factor was injected into the affairs of nations. Until now world peace had been a hope—an ideal, really. But suddenly, overnight, it became the very requisite for human survival. Statesmen and diplomats all over the world were shocked into the realization that the creation of a system of international law and order no longer centered around the question of whether or not it could be achieved at all, but how soon. So the United Nations, which had started out as the latest optimistic exercise in international organization, now became something much more important—man's last desperate weapon against the extinction of the human race.

Early in 1946, the United Nations General Assembly—composed of all members of the international body—created an Atomic Energy Commission to present proposals for the prohibition of atomic weapons, the use of atomic energy for peaceful purposes and the exchange of scientific information. In this way it was hoped that atomic weapons could be outlawed altogether and conventional armaments reduced and regulated.

The United States representative to the UN Atomic Energy Commission was the distinguished elder statesman Bernard M. Baruch. In June of 1946 a plan was submitted to the commission which came to be known as the "Baruch Plan." It was designed to set up a system of international controls. But just as the world began to foresee the beginnings of a new era of international harmony, a deadlock developed among the commission members. The Western democracies, which backed the Baruch plan, maintained that a method of international inspection to guarantee that no country would violate a ban against atomic weapons was necessary before such weapons could be outlawed. The Soviet Union, on the other hand, argued that unlimited inspection would infringe on national sovereignty. It called for an agreement to abolish atomic weapons as a first step toward the adoption of a control system. So bitter was the dispute that the issue remained unresolved.

The divergent points of view between the Communist world and the West soon made themselves felt in other matters as well, and before long a "cold war" developed between the two sides.

Dag, like other Swedish officials, felt that Sweden should follow a neutral course between East and West. Accordingly, trade agreements were signed with Communist Russia and Poland, as well as with the Western democracies. However, Soviet failure to live up to the terms of the agreements eventually led to their virtual abandonment.

In spite of his heavy load of work as adviser to the Cabinet during those early postwar years, Dag kept up with his former interests. He began to develop a taste for modern art, music and poetry, though he also retained his earlier love of the classics. During his initial explorations into modern poetry he discovered the works of T. S. Eliot, the avant-garde American poet who settled in England in the 1920's. Many of Dag's friends argued that Eliot's poetry was unintelligible and expressive of cultural chaos, but Dag himself found in poems like "The Waste Land" a mysticism and emotional identification that he could not fully explain.

For exercise he continued his mountain climbing and skiing and joined the Swedish Mountaineers' Club and the Swedish Tourist Association. When on an outing he habitually dressed in unconventional attire—tennis shoes, sports shirt and shorts.

One weekend, while on a trip to North Sweden, he stopped off at a first-class hotel and asked for a room. The hotel clerk looked down his nose at the slight, sandy-haired figure in canvas shoes and shorts and suggested stiffly that he would do better to try a youth hostel down the road. Dag, without disclosing his identity, left the hotel and proceeded to register at the hostel with a group of teen-age boys and girls who were on a cross-country bicycle trip!

Yet in spite of his full schedule and multitude of activities, there were times when Dag was overcome by a great sense of loneliness. His father, now over eighty-five, spent almost all of his time alone in his study, evaluating the books nominated for the Nobel Prize and saw little of his son except at mealtimes.

During his years in government, Dag had developed a wide circle of friends and acquaintances. Nevertheless, the same sense of shyness that had plagued him as a child continued to deny him the truly close relationship with others for which he had always hungered. Indeed, since the death of his mother he had felt more alone than ever.

The loneliness was at its worst after spending an evening at the home of married friends. He loved children and found that with youngsters he could come closest to revealing his innermost self without feeling embarrassed or self-conscious. For this reason he rarely turned down an invitation to dinner at a home where there were children. He delighted in joining in their games and engaging in horseplay with them. He listened to their youthful problems gravely and played the role of "Dutch uncle" in giving them advice.

After such an evening, as he walked home alone along the chilly streets of Stockholm, he could not help feeling a certain sadness—as if he were being left out of things. In truth, he longed for the warmth of a real home and family.

The thought of marriage had occurred to him often. During his student days he had rarely gone out with girls, but afterward he had had dates with a number of young ladies. His friends, particularly those who were married, urged him to look for a wife. They constantly arranged for him to visit their homes when an unmarried young woman was present.

In truth, Dag had convinced himself that it would be unfair to invite anyone to share the kind of life he led. He often worked twelve or fourteen hours a day, and his duties took him constantly to various parts of Sweden and to other countries. Always on call, he never knew when he might be summoned on an hour's notice to fly to Denmark, Norway, England or Germany—or even to more distant places.

But perhaps the deeper reason was one that Dag hesitated to admit even to himself. As a child he had seen how lonely his mother had been because of his father's constant absences on government business. There were times when they had been separated for weeks or months while Hjalmar Hammarskjold was away on important diplomatic missions. At other times, his work as Governor of Uppland kept him so busy that the family rarely saw him even when he was home. It was this feeling of being shut out of her husband's life that had driven Agnes Hammarskjold, a warm, sensitive woman, to devote most of her attention and love to her children—particularly Dag.

Dag, who had been the closest to his mother and sensed her problems, had possibly developed a deep-rooted fear of marriage and of inflicting on some other woman the loneliness and isolation he himself had witnessed as a child. Nevertheless, he never became angry when friends made crudely transparent attempts to get him to marry. When he showed up for a dinner party at someone's home only to discover that an unattached young lady had been invited, too, he was a perfect gentleman and lavished on her all the little attentions and courtesies he would have shown her had he himself initiated the meeting. Sometimes he would invite her out, and on a few occasions he saw the same girl several times. But invariably, the relationship always seemed to break off before it became serious.

For Europe, 1947 was a critical year. Their resources drained by the war, the countries on the Continent were on the verge of economic, social and political collapse. A program had to be devised to help them get back on their feet, a program that was at once comprehensive and practical. In June of that year, the United States came up with such a plan. Officially named the Economic Recovery Program, it came to be known popularly as the "Marshall Plan," after Secretary of State George C. Marshall who first enunciated its principles. The Marshall Plan called for American aid to European countries to keep them from economic ruin, but it was to be carried out on a "mutual" basis, rather than individually with each nation.

In launching the program, the United States asked the nations receiving aid to accept two responsibilities as a condition for participation. Each country was to help itself to the maximum of its ability, and each was to offer other Marshall Plan nations maximum help.

This was a new concept in international aid programs. For the first time, European countries were to participate as part of a larger community rather than as independent nations. In this respect, the Marshall Plan truly reflected the internationalist thinking of the United Nations Charter, even though it was being implemented outside the UN because of the East-West deadlock.

As part of the program the Marshall Plan countries set up a European adjunct called the Organization for European Economic Cooperation. It was the job of the OEEC to prevent duplication of economic programs and to guarantee that the recipient nations were helping each other as much as possible. Thus it was to serve as a "clearing house" to study and approve requests for aid from the various nations and work out a suitable compromise agreement where there were overlapping programs.

Although Sweden was not one of the countries designated to receive Marshall Plan aid, her role in OEEC was of critical importance. It was felt by the United States and the Marshall Plan countries that as a non-recipient she was in an excellent position to make objective decisions and act as arbitrator where there were conflicting interests.

The Swedish government decided to choose the best qualified chief delegate it could find. His background had to be exactly right if he were to succeed in his difficult assignment. He had to be a gifted linguist and he had to have a superb background in economics. But most important of all, the job called for a skilled negotiator who could encourage the delegates of the other nations to work together harmoniously and get them to compromise where there were disagreements.

From the first there was little question in anyone's mind that Dag Hammarskjold was the man for the job. The government committee designated to make the appointment named him as its unanimous choice. In this role of chief Swedish delegate to the OEEC, he was to hold the rank of Special Adviser to the Ministry of Foreign Affairs.

The meetings of the organization were planned to take place in Paris. Almost upon arrival Dag threw himself into the work of helping to draft an OEEC charter. Here, for the first time, he met leading diplomats from many nations around the same conference table. He got to know them well, to understand their personal quirks and to recognize the areas in which they disagreed with each other.

It has been said that whenever two political economists get together, there is bound to be a difference of opinion. In Paris this was true from the outset. There was a sharp split between the British, supported by the Scandinavians, who believed in economic expansion and full employment, and the representatives of the Continental nations who were more conservative and felt that primary attention should be given to ensuring financial stability and warding off inflation.

Dag, as a Keynesian economist, favored the former policy, but he decided not to press his own view or involve himself in the controversy. He felt that his most important function was to help resolve the disputes, and he knew that as a member of the executive committee of the conference he was in an excellent position to find areas of compromise between the opposing theories.

His old adeptness at tying together a series of complex—even divergent—ideas into concise, logical reports proved to be a key factor. Time and again meetings ended on an angry note only to have the delegates agree to a compromise based on a Hammarskjold-drafted resolution.

Later, a Norwegian delegate, writing of Dag's role at that conference, was to say, "I never heard of anybody who worked with Dag in those years who was not impressed with his capacity to see things in a realistic way, his ability to hold to a neutral position in seeking a solution that would be just in terms of all the interests involved."

But this did not mean that Dag was an agreeable compro-

miser who tried to satisfy everybody. Many times he was forced
to adopt a tough-minded approach and turn down a request
flatly. On such occasions he would set his jaw and reply, "What
you are saying is not reasonable." He used the phrase so often
that some of his fellow delegates began to refer to it as the
Hammarskjold trade-mark. As a child Dag had often heard
his father say, "Being neutral is not a question of saying yes
to both sides, but of saying no to both sides." In Paris he discovered that it was a sound principle to follow.

The Paris conference brought Dag to the attention of some of
the world's leading diplomats. He made a particularly favorable
impression on representatives of Great Britain and France who
had not known him before. Paul Hoffman, the distinguished
industrialist who was serving as United States aid administrator,
described him and Robert Marjolin of France as the "two bright
young men" of the OEEC.

Dag did not know it then, but the reputation he established
in Paris was to have an important effect on his life later on.

Although he followed his previous regimen of keeping long
working hours, Hammarskjold enjoyed every minute of his
stay in Paris. On Friday he flew back to Stockholm to spend the
weekend with his father, but during the week he spent as much
time as he could enjoying the cultural offerings of the French
capital. Very often there would be night meetings scheduled
and at such times Dag and a fellow delegate would have dinner, go to a play and return to the night session to resume business discussions until the early hours of the morning. His companions were invariably taken aback by his ability to pursue
this round-the-clock schedule and yet be clear as a bell at all
times.

On the rare occasions when no meetings were called, Dag
and a few friends would travel through France taking in the
sights. On these trips he would instruct the rest of the party
in French history and culture. "We learned more about the old
churches and cathedrals from him than we could have gotten
out of a guidebook," a fellow delegate said later on.

While the economic negotiations took their slow course in Paris, events of a much more dramatic nature were taking place in other parts of the world. In Palestine an especially tragic situation had been developing for many months.

Exiled from Jerusalem since its fall to Rome in the year A.D. 70, the Jewish people had dreamed for two thousand years of someday returning to the "promised land" of their forefathers. After changing hands many times, Palestine was placed under a British mandate by the League of Nations following World War I.

With the murder of six million Jews by the Nazis, the need for a permanent homeland, where the pitiful remnants of European Jewry could settle, grew into a major point of controversy. The British refused to allow the wholesale admission of European refugees for fear it would lead to trouble with the Arabs. The Palestinian Jews began to organize large-scale illegal immigration in spite of British attempts to blockade the coast.

In the spring of 1947, the British government, unable to maintain law and order and painfully conscious of adverse world opinion, asked the United Nations General Assembly to look into the Palestine question. A special committee appointed by the Assembly recommended that Palestine be divided into an Arab state and a Jewish state and that a special area, including Jerusalem, be ruled under an international government. The plan was accepted by the United Nations.

It was clear that once the British evacuated, there would be trouble between the Jews and the Arabs. To prevent hostilities, the United Nations appointed Count Folke Bernadotte, a member of the royal family of Sweden and president of the Swedish Red Cross, to serve as mediator.

In May of 1948 the British moved out of Palestine. Almost immediately the armies of five Arab nations attacked the new Jewish state. There was bloody fighting as the greatly outnumbered Israelis battled fiercely to defend themselves against the Arab coalition.

Among the victims of the war was Count Bernadotte himself

who was assassinated in Jerusalem. He was succeeded by Dr. Ralph Bunche of the United States, who had been acting as assistant to the Swedish mediator.

By January of 1949 a truce was restored, with both sides agreeing to troop withdrawal and supervision by United Nations observers. Although a final peace settlement was not reached and tension continued, armistice agreements were signed between the Arabs and the Jews. For his work in stopping the war, Dr. Bunche was awarded the Nobel Peace Prize.

During his months at the Paris conference Dag followed the course of the Palestinian difficulties with concern. He felt that it would be an acid test of the effectiveness of the United Nations in mediating disputes.

With the signing of the armistice agreements, he was convinced that the vision of an international organization to maintain world peace was no longer an idle dream.

Chapter Seven

THE DIPLOMAT

When Dag returned to Sweden in 1949 he was amazed to learn that he had been named Secretary-General of the Foreign Office. It was an important step upward. While he was to be in charge of economic affairs, he was to have a direct hand in shaping Swedish foreign policy as well.

The cold war was in its tensest phase. Emotionally and intellectually Dag's sympathies lay with the West, for he was convinced that communism, like fascism, was the antithesis of freedom. In this respect he reflected the thinking of most of the Swedish people. But in spite of his personal feelings he was convinced that Sweden must not allow herself to be dragged into the East-West controversy. He felt that if world order was to be established, the smaller nations must discourage the use of "power politics" that had led to open conflict in the past, and serve wherever possible to promote understanding between the giant powers.

This outlook was traditional among the Swedes. With the oldest written constitution in Europe, they were firm believers in the supremacy of the law as the best safeguard of the rights of individuals. Temperamentally therefore, they were disposed toward a similar development on the international level. They felt that through a body of world laws many international disputes could be solved by arbitration alone. But this could only be done through a "supranational" organization like the United Nations. Furthermore, Dag and his countrymen believed that if Sweden were to ally herself with either the East or the

West on a permanent basis the very principle on which the UN had been organized would be threatened.

So in spite of his own leanings toward the cause of the Western nations, Dag felt that as a molder of Swedish foreign policy he must subordinate his own private beliefs to what was best for Sweden and the world.

He was under no illusions, however, that all disputes could be solved by arbitration. This naïve belief which he had held as a youth, and which his father had tried to discourage, had disappeared with the demise of the League of Nations. As an adult who had lived through two world wars he knew that sometimes solutions could be found only through political negotiation, with legal considerations playing a subsidiary role. Yet here, too, he believed that the best vehicle for political compromise was the United Nations.

Finally Dag knew that instances might arise where neither legal arbitration nor political horse-trading would work, for there was always the possibility that an aggressor nation like Nazi Germany might rise and show its teeth. Such countries had no regard for international law or the rights of other na-tions, and force might have to be used just as officers of the law occasionally have to use force to subdue a dangerous criminal. He felt that if such a need arose, the UN should be the only agency with the right to act as an international policeman.

For these reasons, Dag opposed his country's entrance into the cold war struggle. He was convinced that if Sweden were to play any role at all, it should be that of the intermediary who seeks to reduce friction rather than increase it by joining one side or the other.

As Secretary-General of the Foreign Office it was his job to help formulate policy rather than to announce it. He rarely appeared in public as a spokesman. This role suited him per-fectly, for he had always disliked personal publicity and felt uncomfortable even when his name was mentioned only casu-ally in the press. But inside the Foreign Office he was a key figure. He introduced his own methods of working, including long hours—often ending in the early morning—and constant discussion with his subordinates in order to arrive at sound decisions.

Dag had brought into the Foreign Office a group of brilliant young men who had worked with him in the past. These made up his own private "cabinet." Each issue was debated freely and informally. The Secretary-General's own crackling intellect supplied most of the creative ideas. One of his colleagues said later, "He was like a jet plane. When the sound reached you, the plane already had vanished."

But as he developed each new idea, Hammarskjold liked to try it out on his people, to find the weak points by observing their reactions. Sometimes he would discard an idea, but usually it was so eminently sound that after an all-night debating session the group would agree to implement it almost exactly as Dag had suggested it in the first place.

At first some of the older men in the Foreign Office looked askance at this unorthodox procedure. Traditionally the office had been run along typical bureaucratic lines. Protocol had been observed scrupulously, and the notion of a high official meeting and arguing freely and informally with his underlings was unheard of. But because of everyone's respect for Hammarskjold's trigger-quick grasp of issues and his amazing ability to achieve results, ill will and resentment was held to a minimum. Moreover he kept such a tight reign on things that there was little time for the politicking that customarily took place in large organizations.

As the cold war went on, hopes for a quick settlement of the various disputes seemed to dim. But like many other diplomats Hammarskjold was thankful for the presence of the UN, where the conflict could be fought across a table instead of on a battlefield. One of the sharpest bones of contention was the issue of whether Communist China should be given a seat in the United Nations. The Russians argued that she should be admitted. The West, led by the United States, maintained that the former Nationalist government headed by Chiang Kai-shek, now located on Formosa, was the one entitled to membership. So fierce was the controversy that early in 1950 the Soviet delegate announced that he would boycott future meetings of the UN Security Council to protest the West's refusal to seat Communist China.

In June of 1950 the cold war suddenly grew hot in a remote corner of the world. In an ancient land named Korea, the forces of communism struck directly at the United Nations. It proved to be an acid test of whether the UN would survive or fall apart like the League of Nations.

The roots of the Korean problem lay in the past, for this was a land where misfortune and unhappiness had come to rest like ugly vultures. Conquered and enslaved by Japan in 1910, this sorrowful land had known for decades every evil that could befall a single nation. Following her liberation after World War II, Korea was occupied by the Soviet army in the north and United States troops in the south. In 1948 this temporary occupation became the basis for the creation of two separate countries—a Communist North Korea and a Republican South Korea. The dividing line had been set at the 38th parallel of latitude.

For two years, relations between the two antagonistic governments were strained, often erupting into minor skirmishes along the common boundary. Then, on June 25, 1950, Communist North Korean forces crossed the 38th parallel and attacked South Korea.

On receiving the news, President Harry Truman promptly announced that he would send air and sea forces to help South Korea. He also called upon the United Nations to join in giving military assistance.

The invasion of South Korea was a clear act of aggression, one that the UN would have to meet head on. A resolution was adopted in the Security Council calling upon all members of the world organization to help repel the aggressors. The resolution was made possible only because the Soviet delegate to the

Security Council, who could have vetoed such a resolution, was still boycotting the Council's meetings.

In a short time member nations from all over the world began pouring in troops and arms to oppose the North Korean invasion. It was a significant moment. For the first time in history, countries had joined together under the flag of a world organization to carry out a "police action" against a lawless nation.

The military operations in Korea soon settled into a bloody, drawn-out struggle in which "volunteers" from Communist China bolstered the forces of North Korea. In Stockholm, Dag carefully charted the course of events as the news clattered in on the teletype machines of the Foreign Ministry. But he was also watching another fascinating struggle that was beginning to shape up in the United Nations itself. It was a conflict that in the long run was to prove as significant to the future of the UN and world peace as the Korean police action.

The controversy centered about the role of the Secretary-General of the United Nations, an office that was being filled by a personable, heavy-set Norwegian named Trygve Lie. As head of the Norwegian delegation to San Francisco in 1945, Lie had been one of the founders of the UN. In 1946, he was elected Secretary-General and had served for nearly five years with distinction. Now, a dispute arose that was threatening to undermine the effectiveness of the Secretary-General's role.

In structure, the UN included a General Assembly in which all nations were represented and a Security Council consisting of eleven members, five of which were "permanent." These nations were China, France, the Soviet Union, the United Kingdom and the United States. The other six Security Council members were elected for two-year terms. Decisions of the Council were made by an affirmative vote of seven members. However, except in matters of procedure, the seven affirmative votes had to include those of the five permanent members. Any one of these five member nations could stop a Security Council action by exercising a veto. This provision had been agreed upon in

San Francisco on the theory that any action to safeguard world security would require the cooperation of the five major powers in order to be effective. In actual practice, however, the Soviet Union had used the veto as a weapon to prevent the Security Council from taking action on a great many issues, and this was one of the basic reasons for the deadlock that had developed within the UN.

In addition to the General Assembly and Security Council, the organization consisted of an Economic and Social Council, specialized agencies, the International Court of Justice and the Secretariat.

Thus in structure the United Nations was similar to the League of Nations. As in the League, the Secretariat consisted of a permanent staff headed by a secretary-general who was to serve as the chief administrative officer of the UN. While under the League this official was limited almost wholly to administrative duties, the founders of the United Nations had cast him in a far more significant role. They saw him as an "international statesman" with authority to participate in negotiations and exert influence in all UN activities. Under the Charter he was to be the "chief executive" of the UN as well as its head administrator and coordinator. And he was even given the power to act independently in matters affecting the peace and security of the world.

Trygve Lie had tried to be a strong secretary-general. He had exercised leadership in the Israeli crisis and other problems that had plagued the United Nations since 1946. His efforts on several occasions had brought criticism from some officials in the United States, but because of his strong prodemocratic bias he had stirred up even more antagonism from the Soviet Union. As Secretary-General, he was supposed to keep his personal feelings out of official United Nations business, and he adhered to this policy rigidly. However, at unofficial banquets and gatherings he often delivered speeches in which his own pro-Western viewpoint came out, and this infuriated the Soviets who normally were suspicious of anyone not from a Communist nation.

With the outbreak of the Korean police action, Trygve Lie's position became even more difficult. Although the Soviet Union did not actively participate in the fighting, she gave Communist North Korea arms, ammunition and advice. As the chief executive officer of the United Nations, Lie had been a key figure in urging UN military action against the Communists—thus infuriating the Russians even more. They claimed that in many of his actions he was exceeding his powers as Secretary-General.

In the autumn of 1950, the Secretary-General's term of office expired. Lie was up for renomination by the Security Council, but the Soviet delegate made it clear that he would veto the Norwegian's bid for a second term, and offered to accept almost anyone else as a candidate. The United States representative warned that it would retaliate by using its veto power to rule out anyone but Trygve Lie.

In the end, the General Assembly, which had to vote on the Security Council's nomination, stepped in and broke the deadlock by extending Lie's term for three years without formally re-electing him. The Soviet Union charged that this amounted to re-election and declared it would not recognize the Secretary-General's authority. So even though Lie continued to occupy the post, his effectiveness as an intermediary in the cold war between the East and the West went steadily downhill.

In Sweden Dag Hammarskjold followed every move of the international chess game taking place across the Atlantic in the United Nations headquarters. He felt sorry for his fellow Scandinavian Trygve Lie, although he had never met him personally. He shared Lie's notion of a strong secretary-general's office and felt that any other approach would seriously hamper the effectiveness of the United Nations.

But while he kept track of UN affairs as an interested spectator, he did not neglect his duties in the Swedish Foreign Office. In 1951 he was promoted again—to Vice-Minister of Foreign Affairs and to membership in the Swedish Cabinet, thus becoming one of the nation's most important policy-making officials. As a lifelong student of international relations, it was a role he had dreamed of, though he had never expected to attain it.

In the fall he flew to Paris as Vice-Chairman of Sweden's delegation to the sixth regular session of the United Nations General Assembly. It was his first direct contact with the world organization, and he couldn't help feeling a sense of awe at the burden of responsibility he now shared.

He had thought of the UN as a parliament of nations, and yet it was a parliament of men, too. Men with different colored skins. Men who dressed differently and spoke differently and had divergent philosophies, but who, in spite of differences, were expected to reconcile opposing ways of life around a conference table in a mutual quest for world order and peace.

There were constant arguments and bickering, and sometimes it seemed to him as if the entire task were a hopeless one. There was one depressing evening after an exceptionally stormy meeting in the Assembly when Dag frankly wondered whether the UN itself was not doomed to go the way of the League of Nations, whether man was not by nature destined for perennial conflict and ultimate self-destruction. But finally he decided that if only because of the basic human instinct for survival, the United Nations was bound to succeed in the end. The nations of the world would have to resolve their differences by peace rather than by war. Indeed, with the development of nuclear warfare and its potential for destroying human life completely, was there any alternative?

Upon returning to Stockholm, Dag discovered that the life of a diplomat and cabinet minister was more strenuous than anything he had ever known. Unlike economic planning which was a long-range matter, he now had to make split-second policy decisions, decisions which could have an immediate and lasting effect on the nation.

Even his vacations were no longer his own. In the summer of 1952, he was on a holiday in Lapland, at the same time that

Foreign Minister Osten Unden was vacationing in Italy. For a number of weeks tension between the Soviet Union and the West had been increasing steadily, and Marshal Stalin was issuing violent threats to the entire non-Communist world.

One Friday news went out to the Swedish people that one of their planes had been shot down by the Russians over the Baltic Sea. Two days later, before the people could recover from the shock of this announcement, news broadcasters reported that a second plane had been downed by Soviet fighters.

The normally placid Swedes were infuriated and demanded action. A military plane was dispatched to Lapland to get Dag. It returned with the Vice-Minister and landed at Stockholm, and Dag, still wearing mountaineering clothes, rushed to the Foreign Office to take charge of the crisis in the absence of Unden.

A running propaganda battle between Moscow and Stockholm ensued. Hammarskjold knew he would have to take a firm position, but he also recognized the importance of keeping the situation from taking a warlike turn, though some hotheads were already demanding that the Swedish Air Force fire on Russian planes.

The Soviet representatives in Sweden, long skilled in propaganda techniques, issued their diplomatic notes late in the evening. In this way they hoped to catch the next morning's headlines in the newspapers, before the Swedish Foreign Office had a chance to devise an official reply.

Dag sensed what the Russians were up to and improvised a counter-technique. He and two assistants set up an "all-night watch" to wait for the Soviet notes. As soon as they were received a reply was prepared and rushed off to the papers. As a result, the Russian statements and the Swedish counterstatements appeared in the same editions, thus eliminating the possibility of a Communist advantage.

Night after night the "watch" continued. After a few weeks the crisis eased, but for many months Dag and his colleagues in the Foreign Ministry prided themselves on the fact that they had done what the officials of few other governments had succeeded in doing—outwitted the Russians in a critical propaganda exchange.

That fall Dag was again designated to serve as a Swedish delegate to the United Nations General Assembly meeting, this time as Acting Chairman of the delegation! The meeting, the seventh session of the Assembly, was a historic one since it was to take place in the magnificent new domed General Assembly Building that had just been completed as part of the UN permanent headquarters in New York City.

Dag's first sight of the great rectangular Secretariat Building overlooking the East River almost took his breath away. It was moving and inspiring, this great new citadel in man's battle for peace, and merely to gaze at it from a distance was enough to fill one's spirit with hope.

But in spite of the promise that the new headquarters seemed to hold out, the General Assembly session itself turned out to be a dismal affair. For over a year truce meetings had been held between United Nations representatives and the Communists in an attempt to end the Korean War. It had been everyone's expectation that before the Assembly session ended an armistice would be reached, halting the bitter two-year-old conflict. But in October, word was received that the truce talks in Korea had been broken off because of a failure to reach an understanding on the repatriation of prisoners.

To make matters worse, the United Nations was undergoing a crisis in another area. In the United States Senator Joseph R. McCarthy had created a climate of fear by attacking the loyalty of many United States citizens, including some of its leading public officials. Encouraged by McCarthy's success in exploiting the fear and suspicion of communism for domestic political gains, other American politicians copied his tactics. A Senate committee reported that an investigation of the United Nations had revealed "a new vista of evidence of subversion on the part of United States citizens." FBI agents and Senate investigators invaded United Nations headquarters to obtain information.

Some two dozen American employees of the UN were sub-poenaed by the committee, and they invoked their constitutional right to refuse to testify on charges of past membership in the Communist party. This attack on the organization's integrity dampened morale and resulted in the shocking suicide of one of Trygve Lie's own trusted legal advisors, an American named Dr. Abe Feller, who had found the McCarthy hysteria too much to bear.

On the afternoon of November 10, 1952, Dag and the other delegates to the General Assembly session made their way to their seats and waited for the current president, a Canadian named Lester B. Pearson, to open the proceedings. Seated in his accustomed place at the right hand of the Assembly President was Secretary-General Trygve Lie, his normally expressive face a mask of gloom. And no wonder! He had been attacked as a "stooge" of the United States by the Russians and as "soft on communism" by United States politicians and reactionary segments of the American press. He had seen one of his closest aides take his own life in a fit of despair. His effectiveness as a go-between in the cold war had reached its lowest ebb. Finally he had watched helplessly as negotiations to end the Korean War reached an impasse.

These tragic events, coming one on top of the other, had almost prepared the delegates for what was to happen next. Reading from a letter that he had submitted to the Assembly President the day before, Lie addressed Pearson:

I wish to refer to our personal and confidential conversation on the 11th of September, in which I informed you that I had decided, after lengthy consideration over many months, to submit my resignation as Secretary-General of the United Nations.

Later, Lie was to explain that his decision to resign had been made because:

... it was no longer possible to exercise the political role of the Secretary-General as the Charter had intended, and as I had sought to develop it over the preceding five years. In a world organization where all sides were represented, my hands were tied with respect to governments which controlled or influenced one-third of the population of the world.

Thus, toward the end of 1952, the dream of international understanding seemed more remote than ever. And when Dag Hammarskjold finally flew back to Stockholm he could not help feeling a sense of utter dejection over the state of the world.

Chapter Eight

STATESMAN OF THE WORLD

The months following Trygve Lie's announcement of his resignation was a time of speculation and suspense. In all the capitals of the world statesmen waited and wondered who his successor would be. The rumors and speculation were strongest in New York, of course, because that was where United Nations headquarters was located.

The job of secretary-general was probably the most important diplomatic post in the world. Whoever filled it would help determine the future of the UN itself, and since it was such a critical appointment, the behind-the-scenes maneuvering was bitter and complex.

One of the strongest contenders was Lester Pearson of Canada, the highly respected President of the General Assembly. But he was strongly opposed by the Russians who, because of their antagonism toward the United States, insisted that they would veto the nomination of anyone from North America. Among the other names bandied about were General Carlos P. Romulo of the Philippines and Dr. Charles Malik of Lebanon, both eminently respected diplomats.

As the weeks went by, several things became clear. The Russians, angry at the forceful role played by Trygve Lie, would demand a secretary-general who would limit himself to administration and not interfere in international politics. He would have to be someone from a country not involved in the cold war—a diplomat who would do nothing to offend them or block their attempts to exploit conflict and unrest in the world's numerous trouble spots.

Curiously, the British and French held almost the same view as that of the Russians in this respect. They, too, had not been enthusiastic about the bold role Lie had played. Although the United Nations Charter specifically gave the secretary-general power to take his own initiative in matters threatening the world's peace and security, Britain and France still believed strongly in a quiet, conservative approach to diplomacy. They wanted to get back to the tradition established in the League of Nations, whereby the secretary-general was primarily a high-level administrator, unobtrusive—even anonymous—who would not take the lead or speak out on world-wide issues. They wanted a compromiser rather than an innovator, someone who would not rock the boat of old-style diplomacy.

Only the United States was opposed to this conservative con-cept of the office of secretary-general. Despite past criticism of Lie by some members of Congress and a part of the American press, the United States government was convinced that a strong UN executive was needed to help resolve the multitude of prob-lems that were plaguing the world.

Because of these divergent points of view, the choice of Lie's successor soon reached a stage of deadlock, and as a result the rumors flew thicker than before. The world-wide guessing game reached Sweden, as it did everywhere else. In the Foreign Ministry, Dag and his aides heard dozens of persons mentioned. Some of the names seemed probable choices, others were clearly absurd.

For a brief period there was a flurry of excitement in Stock-holm when a subordinate reported to Dag that there was a strong rumor that Erik Boheman, the Swedish Ambassador to Washington, was being considered. But Hammarskjold pooh-poohed the story, and with good reason. When he had been in New York he had been visited by Boheman's press officer, Sven Backlund, whom he had known for many years. They had had dinner together and discussed the possibility that Boheman might come up for consideration. Backlund had made it clear that in such an eventuality, Boheman would definitely decline.

The rumors continued.

In March of 1953 Dag was asked by officials of the Bank of Sweden to sit for a portrait to be hung in the bank, since he was former chairman of the board. Dag agreed, and one of his artist friends, Bo Beskow, was commissioned to do the job.

During the sittings they discussed the Security Council's difficulty in finding a candidate suitable to all sides. "You know, Dag, you would make a very good secretary-general," Beskow noted casually as he studied the colors on his palette.

Hammarskjold laughed at this preposterous notion. "Nobody would be so crazy as to propose me," he said. "And I wouldn't be crazy enough to accept the job even if anyone thought to offer it to me."

Late the following night, Dag received a strange call from a reporter for one of the news services. He was told that his name was being mentioned as a candidate for the post of UN secretary-general. Did he have any reaction to this?

"Yes," Dag said. "My reaction is a simple one: I don't see why newspapermen should bother to call me at this hour of the night with wild rumors."

"But you see, sir," the reporter protested, "since your name has been mentioned you're 'newsworthy.' "

Dag softened his tone. "Well, I suppose I can see your point of view," he replied. "If you wish, you can say that I'm very much surprised at this curious rumor and find it hard to believe."

On the morning of March 31, Dag showed up at his office as usual and went over the messages on his desk. Among the cables was one from the Swedish delegation in New York City, informing him that a lady in New York—the cable referred to her as a "fussy busybody"—had been publicly backing him as Lie's successor.

Dag smiled and penciled a brief reply to the delegation in New York: "Amused but not interested."

That evening he returned to his apartment and had dinner with his father, but said nothing about the recent events. Just as he was getting ready for bed the telephone started jangling. It was a reporter with some startling unconfirmed "news." The Security Council had secretly voted to submit his name to the General Assembly for the post of secretary-general.

Dag indignantly dismissed the story as speculation and hung up. But the telephone rang again and did not stop ringing for the next hour. Every Stockholm newspaper, as well as the wire services and correspondents for foreign publications, called with the same story—that he was the Security Council's candidate for secretary-general.

He was hurt and angry now. Obviously the story was a lie— an out-and-out fraud. He had received no official message from the United Nations. Not even the Swedish delegation in New York had cabled him. As a diplomat and long-time government official himself, he knew full well that no official body—to say nothing of an international organization like the UN—would release such momentous news without first consulting the central figure in the drama. Suddenly, his eye caught the small calendar and memorandum pad on the table next to the telephone. March 31, it read. And tomorrow would be April 1— "April Fools' Day." So that was it! Someone, somewhere, was playing a gigantic hoax, and *he* had been elected to play the fool. Dismay and bitterness welled up in him now. Even as an April Fool's joke it was a terrible trick to play on a human being, he told himself. Who was responsible for it?

The telephone rang again, and he gloomily picked up the receiver. It was still another newspaper. This caller, an editor, was a long-time friend. He asked Dag if he had heard about the report from New York.

"Yes," Hammarskjold replied unhappily. "But aside from the newspaper reporters, there hasn't been a word from the United Nations. The story is obviously a fraud. It's a cruel joke to play, although if this had been tomorrow—April 1—I might have better understood the motivation of the person who perpetrated it." He said good night and went to bed.

The next morning it was official. The big black headlines in all the Stockholm newspapers told the same story. Dag Hammarskjold had been nominated by the Security Council to become Secretary-General of the world organization. During the early hours of the morning the news had been confirmed by UN headquarters in New York City!

At his office there was a cable waiting for him from Dr. Bokhari of Pakistan, who was serving as President of the Security Council. It was an official message informing him of the Council's action. "In view of the immense importance of this post, more especially at the present time, members of the Security Council express the earnest hope that you will agree to accept the appointment, if, as they hope and believe, it is shortly made by the General Assembly."

Dag was in a daze. His colleagues in the Foreign Ministry congratulated him, and all morning long the telephones rang with messages of congratulations from friends and acquaintances. There was so much turmoil in the Foreign Office that almost no work got done.

Dag was scheduled for a sitting in Bo Beskow's studio, but he and Beskow did little except discuss the job and try to decide what he should do. The Swedish cabinet had already held an emergency meeting and agreed to release him from service. At lunch time he went home and discussed the matter with his father. Hjalmar Hammarskjold, although ninety-one, had strong views on the matter. "Of course you will accept," he told his son. "Your whole life has pointed toward this day."

Dag himself was beset by conflicting emotions. On the one hand he knew that he had no alternative but to take the post as a matter of obligation. Brought up in the best traditions of public service, his deepest convictions would have rebelled at the thought of rejecting this call to duty. And yet, he could not help feeling a curious sense of inadequacy. The job of secretary-general was one of the strangest in the world. It was no simple appointment to higher rank, as his other promotions within the Swedish government had been. To become secretary-general meant a new life, an entirely different outlook. It would mean abdicating his loyalties to the nation of his birth, a nation he had served for more than twenty years, and swearing total allegiance to an international ideal. He would be an international public servant, dedicated only to the concept of world order—regardless of his personal feelings and emotions on any particular issue. It would be a difficult task, this surrendering of private and national interests in favor of the immensely complex needs of all the world's peoples. Was he capable of accepting such a burden?

He recalled the strange story of Thomas à Becket who had changed from a servant of the King to a servant of the Church overnight, and he couldn't help comparing his present predicament with that of Becket. When he had read the story in his youth, he had never dreamed that someday he would find himself in a similar dilemma. The English Archbishop had demonstrated that out of faith in an ideal could come the strength to disavow all personal interests and considerations. And what ideal was more fraught with meaning than that of international order and peace, an ideal which had stirred him all his life?

In his office Dag composed the following cable to the Security Council:

> With a strong feeling of personal insufficiency, I hesitate to accept candidature, but I do not feel that I could refuse the task imposed upon me should the Assembly follow the recommendation of the Security Council by which I feel deeply honoured.

Afterward he went down to a crowded press conference. He apologized for his refusal to comment the night before and explained that he had not known anything about it until his phone had started ringing in the middle of the night. In response to a reporter's question he declared that he was neither "optimistic nor pessimistic" about the post that was to be thrust upon him. "It is the kind of job where one can only do one's best," he said simply. "You can read about its difficulties in the papers."

It had been a busy day. Yet in spite of everything that had happened, Dag could not dismiss from his mind the strange procedure followed by the Security Council in choosing him. Why had there not been official word in advance of the announcement to the newspapers? In disclosing the news before cabling him the Council had taken an awful chance. What if he had refused?

Not until many weeks later did he learn the secret. It was Sir Gladwyn Jebb of Great Britain who disclosed the reason for the Council's unorthodox procedure. The members had felt that if Hammarskjold had been approached by the Council *before* the official vote and public announcement, he would have refused to be a candidate. "We knew for certain you would have said no," Sir Gladwyn told him.

So in the end the members of the Security Council had hit on the idea of voting for the nomination first, *then* releasing the news, so that Hammarskjold would be placed in a position where it would have been most difficult and embarrassing to decline.

Dag was also to learn of the complex series of events and pressures that had led up to his selection. With the United States insisting on a strong secretary-general and Russia demanding a "nonpolitical" official who would be "objective," most of the leading candidates, like Lester Pearson of Canada and Carlos Romulo of the Philippines, had been ruled out because of their identification with a particular side in the cold war. At this point, England and France had stepped in to suggest Dag. To most of the world the name of Hammarskjold meant nothing. Few had ever heard of him and even less knew anything about him. Yet curiously enough, it was this anonymity that stood in his favor.

The British and French diplomats had gotten to know him in Paris during the Marshall Plan negotiations and had been impressed with his razor-sharp mind and his capacity for hard, dedicated work. But to the Americans he was almost unknown. When United States Secretary of State John Foster Dulles first heard of the proposal to nominate Hammarskjold, he was perplexed. Members of the U.S. delegation to the United Nations scurried about canvassing their Scandinavian colleagues. "Who is this fellow Hammarskjold?" they asked. An American diplomat, one of the few who remembered dealing with Dag during the postwar Swedish–United States trade negotiations, told Dulles, "If he's available, grab him."

A hurriedly prepared State Department dossier on Hammarskjold showed him to be an unobtrusive, gifted economist and diplomat, poles apart in personality from the dramatic, flamboyant Trygve Lie. Because of this reputation a few of the American officials feared that he would turn out to be a compromiser rather than a bold creator of policy, and there were a few initial reservations. But eventually they were won over by the high personal esteem in which he seemed to be held by everyone who had ever had any dealings with him.

To the British and French, Dag was the perfect choice, for they were convinced he would subordinate his own role and do nothing to upset any apple carts. The Soviets, although they were aware of Dag's activity in directing the propaganda battle following the Swedish plane episode the previous year, felt that as a career civil servant he could be trusted to take no initiative except when he was specifically directed to do so by the Security Council or the General Assembly.

Strangely enough, most of the behind-the-scenes opposition to Dag's nomination came from Trygve Lie! The plain-spoken Norwegian felt that everything in Hammarskjold's background indicated he was the type of man who would take no risks to defend the United Nations Charter or advance the concept of a strong secretary-general, a concept to which Lie himself had dedicated eight years of his life and which, in the end, had brought about his own downfall.

Lie did not hide his disappointment when he learned that

the Security Council was thinking of choosing Dag. He gloomily told his friends and colleagues, "Any secretary-general who tries to be the kind of officer the San Francisco Charter envisaged will find it impossible to avoid the displeasure of one or more of the greater or smaller states. He will be criticized by right, left and center. Yet because the secretary-general is the servant of the United Nations and not of any single nation, he is obligated to risk himself in the interests of a just solution."

In spite of the retiring Secretary-General's opposition, the Security Council went ahead and nominated Dag Hammarskjold. On April 7, 1953 the General Assembly accepted the Council's nomination and formally elected him to the world's most important diplomatic post.

Chapter Nine

"THE MOST IMPOSSIBLE JOB"

On April 9, 1953, the Terminal Building at New York's Idle-wild Airport was abuzz with newspaper reporters and photographers. Outside, a chilly wind blew in from the nearby Atlantic. A giant airliner slowly pulled up to the arrival ramp and began to discharge its passengers. The newsmen poured out of the building and swarmed around the plane impatiently.

"There he is!" someone shouted. The reporters, photographers and television cameramen descended like a horde of locusts on the slight, blue-eyed, sandy-haired man who climbed down from the aircraft. Flashbulbs popped and the reporters elbowed each other in their eagerness to get as close as possible. Many of them found it hard to believe that this shy, youthful-looking man was the new Secretary-General whom they had been sent to interview.

Dag was met by Trygve Lie who had come to the airport to greet him. The Norwegian introduced him to the press, and the questions began to fly with machine-gun rapidity.

"How do you pronounce your name, sir?"

"Properly it is pronounced 'Hammarshuld,' but it is all right to call me 'hammer shield.' "

"What are your hobbies?"

"Do you like American women?"

"What are your favorite foods?"

Dag was taken aback at the personal nature of the questions and the brashness of some of the American newsmen. He declared that he would not give out information about his private life. "The private man should disappear and the international public servant take his place," he told them.

"How do you conceive your new job?"

"The Secretary-General should listen, analyze and learn to understand the forces at work and the interests at stake so that he can give the right advice when the situation calls for it," Dag replied.

"We understand you like mountaineering. Why?"

"In mountain climbing are required the qualities which I feel we all need today: perseverance and patience, a firm grip on realities, careful but imaginative planning, a clear awareness of the dangers, but also of the fact that fate is what we make it, and that the safest climber is he who never questions his abilities to overcome all difficulties." It was an eloquent statement, and the reporters took notes eagerly.

Dag leaned over to a Swedish associate, Per Lind and muttered, "I hope I can get out of this alive."

The reporters now turned to Trygve Lie and asked him to describe the job from which he had just resigned. The retiring Secretary-General thought for a moment, looked at his successor and said slowly: "It is the most impossible job in the world."

The interview was declared at an end, and Dag and the other dignitaries climbed into limousines and headed for Manhattan whose skyscrapers soon were dimly visible in the distance.

The next day, in the domed Assembly Hall adjacent to the great up-turned slab of a skyscraper that housed the United Nations Secretariat, Dag appeared before the representatives of sixty nations to take the oath of office:

"I, Dag Hammarskjold, solemnly swear to exercise in all loyalty, discretion and conscience the functions entrusted to me as Secretary-General of the United Nations, to discharge these functions and regulate my conduct with the interests of the UN only in view and not to seek or accept instructions in regard to the performance of my duties from any government or other authority external to the organization."

Trygve Lie introduced his successor to the officers of the General Assembly, then escorted him to the dais and indicated the Secretary-General's green marble desk next to the President's. Dag sat down for a moment, then walked to the rostrum to deliver a short inaugural speech. He said, "With humility I accept an election expressing a confidence in me which I have still to justify—with a humility inspired as much by my knowledge of personal limitations as by my awareness of the extraordinary responsibility which you impose on me by your election."

He paused meaningfully, staring out at the sea of intent faces. "Ours is a work of reconciliation and realistic construction," he declared solemnly and concluded with a line from a Swedish poem: "The greatest prayer of man is not for victory but for peace."

During his first hectic days and weeks in office there was so much to do that even Dag felt harried for the first time in his life. Trygve Lie had declared his intention to leave for Norway at the beginning of May. Therefore Hammarskjold tried to spend as much time as he could with his predecessor. On the thirty-eighth floor of the UN Building, in the paneled private office of the Secretary-General, they met with each other daily. Dag asked the stocky Norwegian hundreds of questions and received blunt, unvarnished answers in return.

They discussed every aspect of the UN, and Lie went over the myriad of unsolved problems that awaited solution. Always he was careful not to color his answers with his own philosophy, for he did not want to tell his successor how to do his job. But neither did he try to hide what he felt was the core of the United Nations' problem. "Time is what we need most of all," he said. "Time. Time for the world to condition itself to accept our existence."

What had begun as resentment on Lie's part toward the new Secretary-General turned into a healthy respect as a result of these informal meetings. It was soon obvious that he felt he had unfairly prejudged the mild-mannered Hammarskjold, because he now took every opportunity to make up for his earlier statements of criticism.

"I admire Dag Hammarskjold," he declared to reporters. "I admire his intellect, his knowledge and his administrative ability."

On May 1, 1953, Trygve Lie, with Dag at his side, addressed a final meeting of the UN Staff. "They say the first seven years are the hardest," he told the employees in a moving speech. "I hope for your sake, Mr. Secretary-General, and for your sake, members of the staff, that this saying is true. I do not mind admitting that the past seven years have been hard for me, and I know they have not been easy for you. So before I leave I shall take all the troubles of the past, all the disappointments, all the headaches, and I shall throw them into the East River. I shall carry away with me the memory of all the good things, all the happy things, which have made this job I leave the most satisfying experience of my life. And I hope that you too will remember only the best about our association together."

A week later, Lie sailed home to Norway and Dag Hammarskjold was on his own as the chief executive of the most important organization in the world.

One of his first problems was to establish an understanding with the press. Under Lie the newspapermen were accustomed to receiving dramatic statements almost daily, full of quotable phrases that made the task of the headline writers easy. It was his habit of talking frankly to the press and plunging headlong into political situations that was one of the causes of Lie's ultimate downfall. However, Dag and the explosive Norwegian were as different in temperament as they were in physical appearance. Quiet and unassuming to the point of shyness, Hammarskjold had always been distrustful of the tendency of most of the press to emphasize the sensational. He recognized the importance of a free press in a democratic society, but he also saw that journalistic limitations and the newsmen's need to oversimplify complex events could be dangerous; especially in diplomacy, where discretion and full understanding of issues were essential if international agreements were to be reached free of outside pressures.

During his youthful innocence he had been a firm believer in the Wilsonian concept of "open covenants, openly arrived at." But in maturity he had come to the realization that the principle of "open covenants, secretly arrived at" was a far more effective approach. As a result, he made it clear at the outset that he intended to retain his freedom of action as Secretary-General and would refuse to issue press statements simply to satisfy the needs of the newspapers.

Obviously this did not sit well with many of the reporters. By way of criticism, they accused him of being aloof and even a snob. If such criticism was intended to get him to change his policy, they soon learned that they were up against an experienced, determined administrator who was almost completely unconcerned with personal publicity and press attacks.

Some of Dag's friends were worried about his lack of a "good press" in those early days and called it to his attention. But he dismissed it as of no consequence. "When I accepted this job, I said that in my new official capacity, the private man should disappear and the international public servant should take his place. I mean to stick by that principle."

In only one respect was Dag mildly irritated by his treatment in the newspapers. During the initial interviews he had admitted that he loved mountain climbing and was an avid reader, with a particular affinity for T. S. Eliot. Before long he found himself lampooned in stories and political cartoons which depicted him as carrying an alpenstock—the long metal-pointed staff used by mountaineers—in one hand and a volume of Eliot's poems in the other.

"That's not a picture of me," he complained to colleagues. "It is a caricature. Everywhere I go—mountains, mountains, T. S. Eliot. That's all I hear."

Actually his irritation was directed not so much at the newspapers as at himself for having made the mistake of confiding anything at all about his private life in the presence of newspapermen.

Another of the tasks which Dag considered of front-rank

importance was getting to know his staff. There were more than four thousand United Nations employees ranging from his two top assistants, Andrew Cordier and Ralph Bunche, down to the hundreds of typists, messengers and security guards. He solved the problem by going from floor to floor and office to office, shaking hands with everyone in the huge building. It took two weeks.

At the start he also adopted the habit of eating in the UN's modestly priced cafeteria instead of the more exclusive delegates' restaurant or in one of the finer Manhattan eating places. Although later he had to forego this informality in order to attend important luncheon meetings, he regretted having to give up his cafeteria visits. "You would be surprised how much one learns about the UN by eating in there," he told an aide. "Besides, it's less expensive."

In addition to learning the technical details of his job, Dag had to find a place to live. As secretary-general his salary was twenty thousand dollars a year, with an additional twenty thousand for expenses and fifteen thousand for housing. It was not a large sum, considering the importance of the post and the need to do a great deal of entertaining and traveling. For example, it was far less than the personal funds allotted to the President of the United States—or even to the Mayor of the City of New York. Nevertheless, Dag managed to find a lovely eight-room apartment on Park Avenue, only a few minutes drive to United Nations headquarters.

Instead of hiring a professional decorator, he planned the decoration and furnishings himself. He sent for modern furniture handmade by Swedish and Danish cabinet makers and spent what little spare time he had visiting art shops to choose fine modern prints and paintings to hang on the walls. However, in his living room he installed the ancient desk that had been with the Hammarskjolds for generations. It was his way of retaining sentimental ties with the past and with the family traditions that had been instilled in him as a boy. And on the mantel over the fireplace he placed a model of a Viking ship to remind himself of the proud history of his Scandinavian forebears.

Shortly after moving into the apartment he received a surprising and wonderful gift—an alpinist's "pick" from Tensing, the Nepalese porter who on May 29, 1953, had guided the first party to reach the top of Mount Everest, highest point on earth. On the implement Tensing had inscribed: "So you may climb to even greater heights." Dag mounted the pick prominently over the fireplace, for as a mountain climber himself he considered it a treasured possession.

After introducing himself to the four thousand employees of the United Nations one of Dag's first concerns was how to bolster flagging morale. The attacks by American politicians and press on the integrity of the staff had hurt its effectiveness and efficiency. There were more than 1,680 Americans employed at UN headquarters, many in responsible jobs. While accusations of past Communist affiliation had been leveled against only two dozen, the sensational headlines in the press gave a distorted picture of a world organization whose ranks were riddled with Communists and former Communists.

Trygve Lie, harassed and under fire, had agreed to a request by the recently elected Eisenhower administration to have the FBI check every American on the United Nations payroll. These employees lined up in UN headquarters to be fingerprinted and to answer questions by the federal agents. Henry Cabot Lodge, the new United States delegate, had informed Lie that only in this way could the confidence of the American people in the international organization be restored.

When Dag came on the scene he was shocked at what he considered an unjustified violation of the Secretariat's independence. The concept of an international civil service, he felt, could only succeed if the service were impartial, objective and free of national pressures. The UN employee was theoretically responsible to the United Nations alone and committed only to upholding the Charter. The political investigation of the staff by United States federal agents, carried out with Lie's permission, was a serious compromise of this important principle, Dag was convinced.

Lie himself had come under severe criticism from various delegations and even from his own subordinates for his surrender to the United States' demand. His critics argued that even if there were Communists among the American employees, their continued employment should be based not on standards set up by the American government, but on UN-imposed criteria. If the world organization was to retain its independence, it should be in a position to decide the grounds for dismissal, they maintained.

Therefore, what had started out as a well-meaning attempt by Trygve Lie to restore American confidence in the UN had boomeranged into charges that the organization was subject to McCarthyite pressure and domination by the United States. Moreover, the morale of the staff was at such a low ebb that the Secretariat abounded with unfounded rumors of mass dismissals and wholesale resignations. For the United Nations it was a crucial moment.

Dag's reaction after surveying this unwholesome state of affairs was to term it "a nightmare," particularly the presence of the FBI which he referred to as "absolutely intolerable." Realizing that something had to be done and done quickly, he decided on a bold move. Declaring United Nations headquarters "off limits" to non-UN investigators, he ordered the FBI agents to get out at once. "You can't be here," he told them. "Whatever permission may have been given in the past is withdrawn."

At the same time, Dag was well aware of the danger of antagonizing the United States, whose support of the UN was absolutely vital. So in line with his own background of legal training he introduced a system of judicial procedures within the UN Secretariat to govern the dismissal of employees. In this way standards for employment remained under the control of the secretary-general, free of outside pressures. By the same token the United States government was now satisfied that any American on the UN staff suspected of communism would be investigated by the Secretariat and judicial action taken to dismiss or clear him of the charge.

While the introduction of this new policy eased the immediate crisis, for Dag it raised a number of significant questions. Was an international civil service possible in a world divided by conflicting political ideologies? Could an employee be loyal to the United Nations while at the same time retaining an attachment for his own country? Or were such ties incompatible with the broad international outlook and detachment from national prejudices and narrow national interests needed in a world organization?

Dag knew only too well that such problems touched at the deepest roots of the human personality. Fresh from Stockholm and the Swedish Foreign Ministry he still had to prove to himself that allegiance to the UN and to one's own country were compatible. Since, in a real sense, the future of the world rested on the resolution of this question, he was to return to it time and again in the years to come.

The dismal picture of United Nations prospects faced by Dag when he took office in the spring of 1953 was brightened by an important achievement two months later.

On March 5, word had gone out from Moscow that Communist dictator Joseph Stalin had died of a brain hemorrhage. This news carried important implications not only for Soviet Russia but for the rest of the world. Almost overnight, tensions between East and West began to relax, and for a time it seemed as if the cold war itself would eventually be ended. While this hope proved to be premature, the momentary relaxation of antagonism did help end the Korean War.

The truce talks that had broken off the previous fall were resumed in April, at the request of the Russians. Furthermore, with the departure of Trygve Lie whom the Communists hated and distrusted, the Secretary-General's office was once more in a position to play a role in negotiations between East and West. Dag, realizing his favorable position, worked discreetly behind the scenes to resolve the various difficulties that had stood in the way of an armistice agreement. One by one the issues were negotiated successfully—including the matter of repatriation of prisoners.

On July 27 the Korean police action ended after three years and one month of bitter fighting. Under the terms of the armistice agreement, Korea was to remain divided. So while it did not solve the basic problem of the unification of the country, it did bring an end to the fighting.

The armistice did not satisfy everyone. Sentiment in the United States—which had supplied most of the troops and arms —had been in favor of a decisive victory over North Korea. Within the Communist world, too—particularly in China—the extremists were embittered because the conflict had been stopped before South Korea had been defeated and annexed to Communist North Korea.

Nevertheless, to most of the war-weary world, the coming of a new secretary-general had brought an end to hostilities. Thus Dag's debut on the international scene was considered an unqualified success in most of the capitals of the world, and in the UN itself. He had handled the delicate issue discreetly and effectively, thereby justifying the faith of those who had nominated him for the post. The added status he gained from this initial success was to prove an important springboard for action in the months to come.

On October 12, shortly after the opening of the new General Assembly, Dag received the tragic news that his father had died. Hjalmar Hammarskjold had lived to be ninety-one. He had enjoyed a long and fruitful life. Because of his advanced age, in recent years his sons had been forced to anticipate the possibility of his imminent death. Yet Dag, who flew home to Stockholm to attend the funeral, felt the blow keenly.

Next to his mother, his father had been the most important motivating force in his life. At times the old man had been headstrong, even stern. But in him Dag had always found firm understanding and support. He had passed on to his children the tradition of dedication, loyalty and unswerving integrity that he had inherited from his own forebears. No son could ask more of a father, Dag told himself as he walked moist-eyed along one of Stockholm's ancient cobbled streets after the solemn Lutheran funeral services.

His brothers Bo and Sten tried to get him to remain in Sweden for a few days, but Dag insisted that he must return to New York and the General Assembly meeting. He had long ago found that at times of personal crisis hard work was an infallible remedy for the deep fits of depression that overtook him. Besides, with a dozen international problems before the Assembly, duty clearly demanded that he fly back as soon as possible. He felt that his father would have wanted it that way.

Chapter Ten

APPOINTMENT IN PEKING

At the time of his appointment as Secretary-General, Dag had set up a timetable for himself. Methodical as always, he had approached the new job with the thoroughness of a pilot working out a flight plan. His first order of business, he decided, was to put the UN's administrative house in order. As a result, he had plunged headlong into the task of improving existing procedures in the Secretariat and introducing his own methods of operation, just as he had done in the Swedish Foreign Ministry. In a matter of months he managed to build up strong support and loyalty among his senior staff aides, particularly Andrew Cordier and Dr. Ralph Bunche. These two experienced United Nations hands were amazed at the rapidity with which their new boss managed to grasp the administrative reins firmly and hold onto them.

Dag's free-wheeling method of exchanging views with his assistants at informal *Kaffeeklatsches* initially took some of the United Nations officials by surprise, particularly those with diplomatic backgrounds for whom traditional formality and protocol had been watchwords. But once they got used to his unorthodox way of working they fell right into the spirit and actually enjoyed the give-and-take of frank discussion.

Yet in spite of the informality of staff conferences, Dag studiously avoided establishing close personal relationships with his aides. For one thing, he felt it would interfere with his ability to evaluate them and their ideas objectively. Secondly, his own lifelong characteristic of withdrawing from too intimate relationships with people served as an added buffer.

During discussions of UN business in his thirty-eighth floor office he was friendly and thoughtful. Informality was the keynote. He liked to work with his coat off and his sleeves rolled up. Often, when he wanted to see Cordier or Bunche he would stroll over to their offices rather than summon them through the buzzer. But this informality cut two ways. The Secretariat employees soon learned there was another side to the mild-mannered Dag. Intolerant of stupidity or thoughtlessness, he could be sharp-tongued and angry when he felt the occasion demanded. Sometimes his face would flush red and his blue eyes would turn cold as ice as he lashed out verbally at a sinner who had been irresponsible or needlessly careless. To Dag, praise and criticism were two sides of the same coin, and his own particular code of personal integrity ruled out one without the other.

However, once the business day was over and Dag left the UN Building the relationship ended—until the next morning. For at that precise moment the hidden veil of shyness and loneliness came down, cutting off close personal contact.

While Dag encouraged his aides to submit suggestions and criticism freely, he never permitted himself the luxury of allowing others to make up his mind for him. He examined and weighed points of view carefully, but in the end *he* made the decisions. He heard someone use the American slang expression "passing the buck" and was intrigued with it. On a later occasion, while describing his job to a visitor in his office, he tapped his desk and explained with a smile, "In the UN Secretariat, the buck stops here." Another time, while addressing an audience, he said, "A mature man is his own judge. . . . The advice of others may be welcome and valuable, but it does not free him from responsibility."

According to the operational blueprint he had drawn for himself, it had been his intention to devote his first year in office almost exclusively to internal administrative problems.

"My first job is to run this house," he had said upon taking office. But the unpredictable state of world affairs had thrown his schedule awry, so that by the time he had been in his post only a few weeks he had already found himself elbow-deep in the intricate Korean armistice negotiations.

Fortunately, with the signing of the Korean agreement, the cold war tensions continued to ease for a number of months, thus providing him with the breathing spell he needed in order to return to his original timetable. It was not just his instinctive preference for orderliness that made Dag want to carry out his program as he had drawn it up. There were good reasons why he felt he ought to concentrate on internal administrative problems before embarking on anything else.

He knew that he could not carry out the broader international functions of his office without being able to rely on the support of a well-organized staff. He felt also that unless public confidence in the Secretariat—a confidence that had been undermined by the sniping of American politicians and newspapers during Lie's last months in office—was restored, it would seriously injure the effectiveness of the United Nations.

Except for the Korean negotiations, the UN had been virtually ignored for many months as a device for settling problems. Its influence and prestige were on the wane. The meetings of the Security Council and the General Assembly were being used mainly for propaganda by the big powers. Few of the member nations made a real effort to restore the UN as a vehicle for negotiating differences. On many world issues, the UN was bypassed altogether. Some newspapers and magazines were even making dire predictions that the organization was already headed in the direction of the ill-fated League of Nations.

Dag saw the urgent need to return the UN to the spotlight of world diplomatic activity. And it was to prepare for this major effort that he went to work shoring up the internal structure on which, in the long run, the effectiveness of the world organization depended.

Actually, the Korean armistice had helped restore a little of the UN's faded prestige. Not enough, to be sure; but it *had* served to bolster the sagging morale and self-confidence of the Secretariat officials. And this, Dag felt, was an important gain.

Just as important, it had provided Dag himself with priceless practical experience in UN negotiations. It had opened his eyes, as nothing else could, to the important status of his office and the potential it held for taking the initiative on international issues.

Thus, for the rest of 1953 and well into 1954, while he was hard at work learning the many details of UN organization and operation, he gave a great deal of thought to the role of the secretary-general, based not only on what he had been told by Trygve Lie but on the Korean armistice experience as well.

Lie had been absolutely right in stressing the need for a strong executive, Dag decided. In the final analysis it was the secretary-general who projected the "image" of the UN. World opinion toward the organization could only be as strong as the man who occupied the secretary-general's chair. The delegates themselves were partisan, divided, reflecting the divergent points of view of the nations they represented. To the peoples of the world, therefore, they could never personify the concept of world unity and sense of purpose of the United Nations as an international body. No, it was the secretary-general and his staff, impartial, independent and objective, serving, not the nations from which they had come, but only the UN itself, who most truly symbolized the conscience of the world and the desire of people everywhere for world order and peace.

Dag suspected that it was the lack of a strong and purposeful image that had, in the long run, doomed the League of Nations. The Secretary-General of the League had been an Englishman named Sir Eric Drummond. He had been a remarkably efficient administrator, setting up for the first time in world history the concept of an international civil service. But unfortunately, under the charter of the League, his role was restricted to that of an administrator, with almost no power to initiate action in the political sphere. Thus there had been no strong sense of direction within the League, no one individual who could speak out for an international point of view.

Dag could not help wondering what would have happened if the League had provided for a chief executive with the authority to act on his own, as the UN charter did. Would such power have enabled Drummond to project a more forceful and dramatic image of the League? Would it have prevented the League from going under? Or was it doomed anyway, because of the curious nature of the world itself during those tragic years between the two world wars? It was a fascinating problem, one that ran the gamut of contemporary history, economics and social psychology. Someday, Dag thought, he would want to sit down and write such an analysis.

But at the moment he was certain of one thing. The failure of the League of Nations must not be repeated. The world could not afford it. Like Lie, he was convinced that in the present international picture—a picture darkened by cold war and big-nation deadlock—it was his duty to do everything he could to return the United Nations to the center ring of world diplomacy.

Even before his election as secretary-general, Dag had found himself agreeing in theory with Lie's point of view. Now, having seen the problem close up—having seen it in fact more intimately than any living person except Trygve Lie himself—he realized more than ever the justification for his predecessor's position.

Where, then, had Lie gone wrong? He had exercised dynamic leadership. He had played an active part in resolving the trouble in Palestine and in half a dozen other world trouble spots. He had done a herculean administrative job of trying to transform the UN Charter into an operating organization.

In his frank talks with subordinates and others who had been close to UN affairs since its birth, Dag could not help feeling that one of the problems had been Lie's own personality. He had given the impression of being assertive where he could have been discreet, outgoing and voluble where he should have been guarded. On at least one occasion, notably in Korea, he had even inserted himself into an internal political controversy between South Korean President Syngman Rhee and the South Korean Assembly. This intrusion had drawn sharp words of criticism from all quarters.

In the end, Dag could only conclude that Lie, in his eagerness and anxiety to carry out the task that he had described as "the most impossible job in the world," had tried to move ahead too far, too fast and with too much clamor. It was a mistake he would try not to repeat, Dag resolved firmly.

Throughout the early months of 1954, little happened to alter the world picture. East-West tensions continued, though not as rigidly as in the past. With something approaching a sense of relief, people began to accept the cold war as a normal state of world affairs, as contrasted with the bloody fighting that had recently ended in Korea.

Then, toward the end of 1954, a strange series of events took place that shocked the world into fear and apprehension once more. But it was to prove to be the opportunity Dag had been waiting for to restore some of the United Nation's ebbing influence in international affairs.

On January 13, 1954, during the fighting in Korea, a United States airplane assigned to the UN command in Korea had been attacked and shot down by Communist China. For twenty months nothing was heard about the eleven members of the crew. Suddenly, on November 14, 1954, a news bulletin was issued from Peking, capital of Communist China, announcing that the crew had been sentenced to long prison terms as "spies" for violating Chinese territory. It was also revealed that four other American jet pilots, who had been shot down during the Korean fighting, were being held prisoner.

The United States State Department claimed that the fliers had been shot down over North Korea, not China. It charged Red China with a deliberate breach of international law. The wave of indignation that swept over America and the demands for retaliatory measures were so strong that many observers feared it could lead to another war.

Finally, President Eisenhower, with no other effective course open to him, instructed United States delegate Henry Cabot Lodge to bring the matter to the United Nations. It came up before the General Assembly on December 4.

Clearly the world organization was on the horns of a dilemma. Since Red China had been denied membership in the UN, she was not bound by the Charter and therefore could not be threatened with expulsion for refusing to abide by its provisions. Short of the use of force, it seemed that nothing could be done to get her to surrender the imprisoned airmen.

Nevertheless, a resolution was introduced by sixteen nations condemning Red China for violating the Korean Armistice Agreement. It also requested the Secretary-General, acting in the name of the United Nations, to make "by the means most appropriate in his judgment, continuing and unremitting efforts to obtain the release of the captured airmen." After several days of debate, the resolution was passed overwhelmingly by the Assembly.

The second half of the resolution, asking the Secretary-General to act, dismayed Dag. In effect, the delegates were throwing up their hands and telling him, "We don't know what to do next, so we're tossing the hot potato in your lap."

He felt it was unfair to instruct him to take action in such vague terms without even the hint of a suggestion as to how they expected him to proceed. Besides, if he were to send a note to the Red Chinese and be rebuffed, it would further damage the UN's prestige.

Dag couldn't help feeling that he had been caught in a maze, with no way out. During the next few days he pondered the problem from all sides, desperately hoping that a solution would turn up.

Then a daring plan began to shape itself in his mind. The idea came to him late one night, after he had gone to bed, but once kindled it fired up his brain so he couldn't sleep.

Early the next morning he called Hans Engen, the permanent delegate from Norway, with whom he had become friendly.

Engen came to his office and over coffee they discussed the Assembly resolution and its implications.

Finally Dag leaned back in his chair, lit a thin black cigar and took a deep puff. "What would you say," he asked Engen quietly, "if I were to tell you that I intend to go to Peking to see about the release of those fliers?"

The Norwegian, an exuberant blond-haired man, whistled. Then, after thinking for a long moment, he outlined the risks. What guarantee was there that the Chinese would see the Secretary-General? What if they were to agree to the visit, then turn down Dag's request for the airmen's release? Indeed, in their anger at being denied admission to the UN they might do just that—as a means of embarrassing the world organization.

Dag had anticipated these objections. He readily acknowledged that the dangers Engen had suggested were real ones. But he also pointed out that it was significant that the Chinese Communists themselves had released the news of the trial and the sentencing of the prisoners. "Those people rarely do anything without a reason," he explained. "If they were not ready to negotiate they would have kept their action a secret, and no one would have been the wiser."

Engen conceded that Dag's reasoning made a good deal of sense.

"Besides," the Secretary-General added, "I have been directed to do something. What other effective avenue of action is open to me?"

Once his mind was made up, Dag worked fast. First, he decided *not* to send the text of the General Assembly resolution to Peking. He felt that since it was a statement of condemnation it would only make the Red Chinese leaders feel that they had "lost face," thus constituting an added roadblock to negotiation. His strongest weapon, he decided, was his own status as Secretary-General. The Chinese were too shrewd not to realize that a gratuitous rebuff to the chief executive of the world organization might close the door to future membership even more tightly.

He now sat down and composed a carefully worded cablegram to Chinese Premier Chou En-lai. He mentioned the "special responsibility" the Assembly had given him with regard to the imprisoned fliers and added: "I would appreciate an opportunity to take this matter up with you personally. For that reason, I would ask you whether you could receive me in Peking. I would suggest a visit soon after December 26 and would, if you accept my proposal, ask you what date at about that time would be suitable to you."

Then he settled back to wait for a reply. None came that day. Nor the next. Nor the day after that.

Dag grew anxious and worried. What if the attempt had failed? Since this was his first major diplomatic assignment—even though an almost impossible one—his entire career was at stake, in a sense. But even more critical was the danger of a further blow to United Nations prestige at a time when it simply could not afford a failure.

Finally, a week after he had cabled his message to Peking, a reply arrived from Premier Chou En-lai. Two came, in fact! Both cables arrived within half an hour of each other. The first read: "In the interest of peace and relaxation of international tension, I am prepared to receive you in our capital, Peking, to discuss with you pertinent questions." But the second cable was ambiguous. It declared that there was no justification for the UN to interfere in an internal affair such as the punishment of spies by the Chinese government.

In spite of the apparent contradiction in the messages, Dag knew that at this point there was no turning back. The Chinese had accepted his request for a visit, and he could not now change his course.

News of the impending visit to Peking by the Secretary-General raised a storm of comment when it appeared in the press. Even though the details of the trip were vague and Dag himself did not know what to expect, extremists in the United States were quick to condemn him for being ready "to pay a ransom to the blackmailers." The bulk of public opinion, how-ever, reflected a "wait and see" attitude.

Dag was frankly embarrassed to find himself the central figure in the unfolding drama. He had made up his mind to avoid the spotlight, to do his job quietly and behind the scenes. In fact he had made a firm resolve to avoid casting himself in any dramatic role. Yet here, on his first big assignment, he suddenly had become the key actor. In planning the visit he somewhat naïvely had assumed that it could be arranged and carried out confidentially, without public fanfare. Clearly, he had underestimated the dramatic impact such a trip would have on the public.

As he went ahead with the details of the trip, he made every effort to ignore the press which now dogged him every hour of the day and night in the hope of obtaining further information. Whenever he left his office reporters trailed on his heels, and some even camped on Park Avenue outside the building in which he lived, in the hope that he would say something quotable. Unfortunately, the more tight-lipped he was about his coming mission, the more the interest of the press and public was aroused.

Many weeks before his decision to go to China, Dag had received word from Stockholm that he had been elected to his father's seat in the Swedish Academy. The installation was to take place on December 20, and the Secretary-General had promised to be there. As it turned out, this arrangement coincided beautifully with his plans for the Peking flight. Since the Chinese Reds had an ambassador in Stockholm but none in the United States, the trip would enable him to work out with the Chinese Ambassador to Sweden the details of the Peking journey.

Dag flew to Stockholm the second week in December and held a series of private conferences with the Chinese Ambassador, General Keng Piao. They discussed the route to be taken, the duration of the visit and the conference procedure to be followed with Premier Chou En-lai.

On December 20 Dag attended the solemn installation ceremony at the Swedish Academy of Letters. In the presence of the assembled members, the Secretary of the Academy carefully removed a large blue volume from a box, opened it and indicated the parchment pages on which were engraved the statutes set forth by Gustavus III in 1786 when the Academy was founded. "Do you accept these statutes?" he inquired gravely.

Dag replied that he accepted them, whereupon the Secretary asked him to signify his acceptance by signing a companion red volume. The Secretary-General penned his signature slowly and deliberately in bluish-green ink under that of his father and then proceeded to a chair numbered XVII, which had been his father's and was now his. His installation address to the assembled members was a moving eulogy of Hjalmar Hammarskjold. Dag acknowledged his deep debt to his father and the family tradition of dedication and purpose which the older Hammarskjold had instilled in him. "Between the nation in history and the individual, the family is the primary tie," he declared.

Two days later, he was back in New York. Unable to hold the newsmen at bay any longer, he reluctantly agreed to attend a press conference. The room was filled to overflowing with reporters and cameramen. The questioning was pointed. It was clear from the inquiries of a few of the correspondents that some American newspapers were still critical of the trip. They felt it was an act of "softness" toward Red China. Other reporters demanded to know if Dag was going in order to offer Peking a UN seat in return for the release of the airmen.

The Secretary-General replied flatly, "I am not going anywhere to beg for anything." But on the actual details of the trip itself he refused to divulge any of his plans.

Departure for Peking had been set for December 30. The night before departure, the Soviet delegation amazed everyone by throwing a farewell party for Dag to which all the United Nations delegates were invited. It was all the more surprising since the Russians had vetoed the very resolution condemning

Red China and directing the Secretary-General to take action.

The next morning, a large contingent of UN delegates and employees braved a cold, biting wind to go to the airport to wish Dag and his small party a safe journey. In addition to Dag, the party consisted of Dr. Ahmed S. Bokhari, a political adviser; Professor Humphrey Waldock, adviser in international law, Per Lind, the Secretary-General's executive aide; Gustav Mystrom, a Swedish Lutheran missionary who was to act as interpreter; William Ranallo, a husky UN security officer who served as Dag's personal bodyguard; and Miss Aase Alm, a secretary.

The huge U.S. military Constellation which was to carry them on the first part of the journey came to life with a defiant roar, raced down the runway and nosed into the air like a graceful eagle.

The initial leg took them to London where they stopped over for a full day before climbing aboard a chartered plane for the long, tiring hop to New Delhi, India. The final leg, from New Delhi to China, took them over vast plains and past great snow-capped Himalayan peaks so magnificent they took Dag's breath away.

As a mountain climber he had read many books about these majestic mountains and seen hundreds of photographs, but he realized now that trying to describe or picture them with a camera would be hopeless. For sheer, rugged beauty the Himalayas surpassed anything he had ever seen. He remembered Tensing's alpenstock hanging over the fireplace in his apartment and wondered silently about the thrill of climbing such mountains. Surely, to triumph over them must give the greatest satisfaction in the world, he told himself.

They arrived in Canton, China, early the next morning.

Chapter Eleven

RETURN TO THE WEST

The huge transport broke out of a bank of thick clouds, circled the Canton airport once and dropped gently onto the runway for a perfect landing. The rolling hills surrounding the city presented a picture postcard view as Dag and his party climbed out of the aircraft.

It was a cold morning and snow was falling steadily. They were met by a representative of the Chinese Foreign Ministry who took them to a hotel in the city where they were joined by two interpreters for lunch. That afternoon they boarded a Chinese plane and headed north for Hankow where they spent the night. Dag visited the Swedish Consulate there and spent time with his nephew, Peder Hammarskjold, who was serving as Chargé d'Affaires.

The next morning they flew due north again, reaching Peking before noon. The temperature in the capital was fifteen degrees below zero when they landed, and an icy wind swept down from the Mongolian plains. Yet in spite of the bitter cold, a huge contingent from the Chinese diplomatic corps was on hand at the airport to greet them. By the time the round of handshaking was completed, Dag's party was nearly frozen.

Arrangements had been made for Dag and his personal assistants to stay at the Swedish and Norwegian Embassies. The rest of the UN party was put up at the Peking Hotel.

After lunch they paid a short courtesy call on Prime Minister Chou En-lai who welcomed them to Peking, the Heavenly City. Like Dag, Chou was of aristocratic origin. In his mid-fifties, he was a "patrician Communist," with exquisite Oriental manners and the ancient subtlety of his people written in his face and in every movement of his hands.

The Chinese leader greeted Dag cordially and they chatted briefly about the flight and the weather. That night there was an elaborate reception in a magnificent room known as the Hall of the Purple Light.

The first formal meeting between the Prime Minister and the Secretary-General was held the next day. It lasted three and a half hours and took place in a large conference room known as the Hall of the Western Flowers.

Dag and Chou sat in the middle, flanked by their teams of aides. The Secretary-General noted with interest that all the Chinese—including the Prime Minister—were dressed alike, regardless of station. Their clothes were blue, consisting of a coat buttoned up to the neck and a jacket and trousers of quilted cotton or woolen serge. Later, however, he learned that the reason for this uniform garb was not so much the concept of Marxist egalitarianism as the bitter cold.

Throughout the lengthy discussion, tea was served frequently in tall, lidded Chinese cups. The tea was of a delicious, light-bodied Chinese variety, served with platters of cookies. Except for the voice of the person speaking, an eerie quiet pervaded the Hall of the Western Flowers. Even the servants who brought in the tea performed their tasks in absolute silence.

Chou followed the tradition of Oriental diplomacy by speaking in indirect and carefully circumscribed terms. It was necessary to read in between the seemingly innocuous sentences to understand what he was really saying. Even Dag, who had been accustomed to hearing the language of diplomacy all his life, was awed by the skillful conversational subtlety of the Chinese Prime Minister.

Sensing that the same indirectness was expected of him, the Secretary-General played the game to the hilt. He cloaked his own statements in complex circumlocutions, taking care never to say outright what was on his mind. They spoke through the interpreters, discussing not only the airmen but a variety of Far Eastern problems. The Secretary-General pointed out that while the Chinese considered the issue of the imprisoned airmen a

domestic matter, its effects could have serious international repercussions on the peace of the world. It was for this reason
that he had decided to make the long and difficult flight to
Peking.

To Dag's surprise, Prime Minister Chou readily accepted this
argument and admitted that Dag's concern was a legitimate one
and that he had every right to bring it up. Moreover, the Chinese leader declared that his country recognized the UN Charter
even though it was not a member of the world organization!

Three more conferences were held during the next four days.
In all, the conversations totaled more than thirteen and a half
hours. At the end of each, a brief joint communiqué was issued
by the Peking government and the United Nations representatives, but these gave only the time of the meeting, the date
and who participated. Nothing was released about the nature
of the talks themselves.

As the scope of the discussions broadened, the Secretary-General got the impression that the Prime Minister feared an Amer-
ican-backed attack on the Chinese mainland from Formosa or
South Korea. Trouble had been brewing in the Formosan Straits
for some time. In fact, it was one of the chief causes of friction
between Red China and the United States. Therefore, Dag
considered it important to know that the Chinese took the
possibility of an attack seriously—or at least gave that impression. He felt that if the real cause of tension were known,
efforts could be made to reduce it.

Dag now laid before Chou the entire case for release of the
captured airmen. He explained the advantages of such a move
in easing the threat to world peace. The Chinese Prime Minister couched his answer with great care. While he made no
specific promise, he implied clearly that he was not against
making such a conciliatory move, provided it could be done so
that China would not "lose face" by appearing to give in to
pressure.

At the conclusion of the final day's talk, the joint communiqué stated: "In these talks reference was made at the same time

to questions pertinent to the relaxation of world tension. We
feel that these talks have been useful, and we hope to be able
to continue the contact established in these meetings."

In between the formal conferences with Chou there were
dinners and receptions. The menus included consommé of swal-
lows' nests, Peking duck, lotus seed soup and Mandarin fish.
There were also visits to Chinese palaces and temples and an
excursion to tombs of the Ming Dynasty, which Dag, who had
read a number of books on Chinese history and culture, found
fascinating.

The UN party was scheduled to leave Peking on January 11.
On the eve of departure, the Prime Minister held a final ban-
quet in Dag's honor. It consisted of thirty-six courses!

During the flight back to India, the Secretary-General discussed the talks with his aides. They agreed with him that Chou
meant to free the fliers. But when?

"My guess is six months," Dag said. "They will need that
much time so it will not appear that they are yielding to pressure. The important thing is not to indicate publicly what we
expect the Chinese action will be, or it will jeopardize the
whole operation."

Upon arriving in Kowloon, China, the UN party was be-
sieged by more than a hundred reporters pleading for information. Dag issued this prepared statement:

> I am not willing to reply to any questions, but I could say
> a few words. You certainly appreciate that this is neither
> the time nor the place for me to make any comments on
> my talks in Peking. You will know that I am requested to
> report to the General Assembly on my efforts.

His statement also included a warm expression of appreciation to the Chinese government for its hospitality and cordiality.

When the wire services carried Dag's words to the American
press, reaction was mixed. Undoubtedly everyone had hoped
he would say what they would have liked him to say—that he
had obtained the unconditional release of the fliers. Neverthe-

less, the majority of observers and editorial writers urged patience and resoluteness. Even U.S. Secretary of State John Foster Dulles, no friend of the Chinese Communists, urged the American people to be "slow to anger" and stated that he was eagerly awaiting Dag Hammarskjold's report on a mission that "critically involves issues of humanity and justice."

But the newspapers and commentators who had been critical of the visit before it took place, now attacked it even more bitterly. They dismissed the notion that anything good could have come out of it and asserted that Dag undoubtedly had been sold a bill of goods by the treacherous Chinese.

Although these voices represented a minority, they were loud enough to worry the UN officials in New York. They got in touch with their boss en route from India and explained the situation to him. He authorized the press office at United Nations headquarters to issue a statement taking note of the reports that he had failed in his mission, and to state that the Secretary-General "had not failed" but that it would be necessary to "give it a little time."

Two days later, Dag landed at Idlewild Airport in New York City and that same afternoon he was in his Park Avenue apartment discussing the trip with Henry Cabot Lodge, United States delegate to the UN. The Secretary-General reported that he had every reason to believe the fliers would be freed, but that the Chinese would have to find a device to "save face," for in the East the concept of "face" was exceedingly important. He also informed Lodge of Chou's alleged fear of a U.S.-sponsored military and naval action from Formosa or South Korea on behalf of Nationalist China.

At the conclusion of their talk, Lodge told the press, "There is, naturally, disappointment that the immediate release of our fliers was not effectuated, but I am confident that progress has been made and that our fliers will be free. . . . We must have both patience and determination."

On January 18, five days after Dag's discussion with the American UN delegate, Secretary of State Dulles held a press

conference in Washington, D.C. He announced that the United
States would welcome the idea of having the United Nations
work out an agreement to reduce tension in the Formosan
Straits. The following day, President Eisenhower endorsed the
Dulles proposal at his own press conference. It was a definite
softening of the previous United States position.

When Dag read these stories in *The New York Times* he was
delighted. He knew that the Red Chinese would see it as a
conciliatory gesture and interpret it as meaning that the United
States did not intend to launch an attack on the Chinese mainland. His strategy as an intermediary between the two hostile
sides was beginning to pay off!

But as the weeks passed and there was no indication of Chinese intent to release the airmen, the editorial clamor for
drastic action continued. Meanwhile, behind-the-scenes efforts
on behalf of the prisoners were also being made by Krishna
Menon of India who had visited Prime Minister Chou En-lai
as a special emissary from Indian Prime Minister Nehru.

By April tensions between the United States and Red China
were beginning to increase once more. Fearful that the progress
already made would be lost, Dag decided to fly to Stockholm
to see General Piao, the Chinese Ambassador to Sweden. In
order to keep the real nature of his flight confidential, he announced to the press that he was planning to attend meetings
of the Swedish Academy.

In Stockholm, he met secretly with Piao and pointed out that
in Peking he had considered the matter of the airmen settled,
except for China's need to delay their release until a more
strategic moment presented itself. In view of the worsening
relations between China and the United States, time was running out, he warned. The General conceded that Dag's analysis
made sense and promised to see what could be done.

Before leaving Stockholm, the Secretary-General told friends
that he would return to Sweden in the summer for a vacation.
"I intend to be here for my birthday," he promised.

This casual remark, as Dag learned later, was to have an important consequence.

A short time after his departure from Sweden, one of his friends, Uno Willers, attended a party in Stockholm and met a representative of the Chinese Embassy. The Oriental diplomat learned of the Secretary-General's vacation plans. Later, Willers received a call from the Chinese Embassy itself. "I would like to know the birthday of Mr. Dag Hammarskjold," the caller requested. Willers informed him that it was July 29. The man thanked him and hung up.

On May 30, five weeks after Dag's meeting with General Piao, the Peking government announced that it would release the four jet fliers who had been held prisoner along with the eleven other airmen. The Chinese statement said: "All the evidence is conclusive and irrefutable and the defendants deserve the full punishment prescribed by law, but taking into consideration the fact that the defendants were only carrying out the orders of the military authorities and have all admitted their crimes . . . they are therefore being treated with leniency."

At this news, Dag felt quietly jubilant. Prime Minister Chou En-lai was beginning to carry out his implied promise.

But instead of subduing the critics of the Secretary-General's visit to Peking, the Chinese action was viewed by them as a vindication of the "get tough" policy they had advocated. "Where are the other eleven fliers?" they demanded. Having convinced themselves that the Chinese had released the four airmen out of fear of U.S. military might, they now called for stronger threats to force Chou to free the other prisoners.

"One of the most curious and upsetting things about the present world situation," Dag observed to an aide, "is that everybody distrusts and fears everybody else."

As spring turned into summer and New York City sweltered in the heat of a scorching July, activity at United Nations headquarters slowed to a standstill. Most of the Secretariat employees left for vacation. After attending to some last minute administrative duties, Dag packed his luggage and boarded a flight from Idlewild to Sweden.

After spending a few days with friends in Stockholm, he went to Loderup, a small village in the south of Sweden, to read and rest and spend time with his artist friend Bo Beskow and Bo's young wife Greta. On July 29, the Beskows gave a little party in honor of Dag's fiftieth birthday.

Two days later, a messenger tracked the Secretary-General down and handed him an official communication. It was from the Red Chinese government informing him that in a few days the eleven remaining airmen would be released! But the message was careful to point out that the action was being taken, not because of the resolution of the General Assembly, but out of personal regard and friendship for the Secretary-General. It ended by extending warm congratulations on his birthday.

As he read the communication Dag was deeply moved. He handed it to Bo Beskow without a word and lit a thin black cigar with hands that trembled slightly.

The artist realized immediately the tremendous significance of the message. He knew that as soon as the news was released the press would be down in droves. "How would you like to do a little fishing?" he asked Dag slyly. "The water is one place the newsmen can't get to you—unless they are willing to swim for their statements."

They rented a boat in the village, packed it with fishing gear and sandwiches, and Bo, Greta and Dag spent the day fishing, reading and sunning themselves.

The water glowed golden from the late afternoon sun when they finally headed back for shore. As the small craft nosed into the boat channel, an amazing sight met their eyes. On the dock and on the surrounding hills—as far as the eye could see—there were people. Men, women and children by the hundreds. In their hands they carried little flags which they waved at Dag as they made the hills ring with their cheers. And in the faces of some there were tears of joy.

The happy news had reached Loderup.

Chapter Twelve

THUNDER IN THE MIDDLE EAST

Dag's amazing triumph of personal diplomacy had an immediate and dramatic effect. In diplomatic circles he was hailed for his determination, balance and discretion. Naturally, the intimate details of his complex negotiations with China and the United States remained confidential, so that the general public was unaware of the drama that had taken place behind the scenes. However, in the UN itself and in the world capitals, statesmen and other professional observers of international events knew from the results that he had done an extraordinary job.

To the United Nations, Dag's success proved to be a shot in the arm. Member nations who had reluctantly concluded that the UN was ineffectual now had second thoughts. They saw what they had failed to see before—that by giving broad powers to the Secretary-General the UN Charter had provided a trump card. Even where the Security Council was split and could not act on a threat to world peace because of the threat of a veto, the Secretary-General could step in to fill the breach. Moreover, they knew that in Dag Hammarskjold they had a resourceful executive. As an exponent of "quiet diplomacy" and behind-the-scenes negotiations, he could work effectively to arbitrate disputes without the parties involved risking the embarrassment of "losing face" or prestige—an ever-present danger when a dispute was aired in public debate.

The member nations thus began to see the UN once more as an agency with a potential for settling international problems. True, as realists in international affairs, the diplomats did not delude themselves into thinking that a panacea to world problems was at hand. With the cold war still in progress, the East-West deadlock in the Security Council continued to present a serious problem. Even Dag recognized that a real solution to basic issues would have to wait on improved relations between Russia and the West. This would take time. But at least there was now the hope that through the office of the secretary-general some progress could be made in settling immediate threats to world peace. And the introduction of hope, where there was almost none before, was a step in the right direction.

This renewed faith in the United Nations communicated itself to people everywhere. When the UN had first been organized it represented the dream of hundreds of millions, a dream that had come close to being shattered in the years of East-West bickering and conflict. It was the dream of the peasant whose crops and land had been devastated by warring armies; of the soldier whose legs had been blown off by a mortar shell, of the concentration camp refugee whose family had been wiped out in the gas ovens. It was the dream, too, of a little carpenter—a victim of Fascist oppression—who in 1946 had lovingly fashioned the first ballot box used by UN delegates and whose daughter had dropped into the box a note that read: "The hopes of the world go into this ballot box. I pray that the member nations will remember the people when they cast their votes."

It was important, then, that the faith of the people be restored in the UN. And what Dag had achieved as a result of those difficult months of negotiation on the prisoner issue was just that. Nothing that the world organization had accomplished up to that time had so captured the imagination of humanity. In effect, he had laid the groundwork for a resurgence of UN prestige and influence—ingredients vital to its future success.

In the months following the Peking announcement Dag continued working with no letup. The pace he set was followed enthusiastically by his subordinates. Within the Secretariat it-self morale was higher than in years, and it was due almost wholly to Dag's diplomatic success. Among his aides there was a growing loyalty to the "chief" that made it possible for him to drive them almost as relentlessly as he drove himself.

There were endless duties for the Secretary-General to per-form. In addition to serving as chief administrative officer for all meetings of the Security Council and General Assembly, he also acted in a similar capacity for meetings of the UN Trusteeship Council and the Economic and Social Council. Each year he was expected to submit a report to the General Assembly on the work of the United Nations. And he was required, too, to coordinate the work of UN employees in Geneva, Bangkok, The Hague, Montreal, Santiago de Chile and other places where specialized agencies or branches of the organization were located.

In 1955 Dag was called upon to initiate an important step forward in an area that had plagued mankind for a decade, ever since the moment that the first atomic bomb had fallen on Hiroshima. He was given a mandate by the General Assem-bly to organize an unusual conference in Geneva, Switzerland —a meeting that hopefully would pave the way toward inter-national control of atomic energy!

Back in December of 1953 President Dwight D. Eisenhower had addressed the General Assembly, calling attention to the danger of human annihilation by atomic and hydrogen bombs. He had suggested an unprecedented "Atoms for Peace" plan to eliminate the growing danger of uncontrolled nuclear arma-ments.

The President had proposed that the nations with atomic ma-terials contribute some to an international pool operated by a projected International Atomic Energy Agency under the sponsorship of the United Nations. After a year of East-West bickering the General Assembly passed a resolution on Decem-ber 4, 1954, endorsing such an agency and instructing the

Secretary-General to set up the first International Conference on the Peaceful Uses of Atomic Energy.

Working quickly with the able assistance of Dr. Ralph Bunche, Dag organized preliminary meetings to set up an agenda for the conference. It was no easy task, for representatives of both East and West would attend, and every detail had to be worked out carefully. The stakes were high. If the conference failed it would be a powerful argument against similar meetings in the future, and the atomic issue would remain deadlocked, with mankind's fate hanging precariously in the balance.

When the conference finally was held in August, 1955, the leading scientists of more than seventy nations were present. Even the most optimistic expected initial distrust and conflict, for in the past many East-West meetings called to resolve even simple diplomatic procedures had broken up in an angry atmosphere of charge and countercharge.

But this time it was different. The representatives were scientists, not diplomats. And even hostile nations found that through the language of science there was a common means of communication and understanding. Soviet and American scientists met, discussed and compared notes. They presented papers on findings and techniques and exchanged ideas on the course of future laboratory investigations. They conferred on the application of nuclear energy to medicine, farming and industrial production, and they forecast the coming of a peaceful atomic revolution that would dwarf man's past scientific accomplishments. When the conference came to an end, the proceedings of the various meetings and the texts of the scientific papers were sufficient to fill sixteen printed volumes!

Afterward, in analyzing the success of the conference, Dag saw it as a new kind of cooperation among those working in the atomic field. True, no steps had been taken toward the control or elimination of nuclear armaments. But he couldn't help thinking that through the exchange of knowledge and ideas in the peacetime uses of the atom, the nations were really laying the groundwork for future action in the control of armaments as well.

Control of nuclear weapons, Dag was convinced, would not come about overnight. It would take time. There would be continuing distrust and recrimination. But eventually progress would come. It *had* to come if civilization were to survive. There would be those who would be discouraged easily, and others who would oppose negotiations and concessions on the grounds that it would make their side temporarily vulnerable. Yet ultimately, out of this first successful conference, would come the thread of continuing discussion and step-by-step progress, with the United Nations serving as the catalytic agent.

The following year a statute was signed by eighty nations setting up an International Atomic Energy Agency as the first practical step toward world control of atomic energy!

In spite of his long hours at the UN, Dag managed to keep his private life intact. Except during times of crises, when he would work until all hours with little or no sleep, he geared his schedule to leave his office at eight in the evening. After dinner he would read for at least an hour, for he found in literature a form of intellectual therapy. "If one reads only UN reports, one would develop a rather curious mentality," he wryly told a visitor one day. As always, his reading covered a startling variety of subjects and authors. They included Thomas Wolfe, Marcel Proust, John Steinbeck, Thomas Mann, St.-John Perse and, of course, T. S. Eliot. In addition, as a member of the Swedish Academy, he was required to keep up with the books of authors who were likely candidates for the Nobel Prize in Literature.

But he also enjoyed reading the works of contemporary philosophers like André Gide and Martin Buber. He was particularly fascinated by Buber. This little-known Hebrew sage was a clarion voice, calling for individual responsibility in a complex world where people lose heart and abdicate their will before the monolithic power of a state or a corporation or a political party. The community, Buber had written, is the highest form of social development, but it is a true community only when the people who belong to it retain their individual identities and respond to each other as "openhearted" individuals, responsive to each other's needs.

It was a highly complex philosophy, this concept of Buber's, yet in it Dag saw the spark of his own life's goal. What else was he attempting to accomplish but to hasten the day when the nations and peoples of the world would comprise a real community of mankind?

Dag did not restrict himself to sedentary activities, however. Ever restless and bristling with physical energy, he discovered soon after settling in New York that he missed the rugged north country of Scandinavia and his weekends of mountain climbing and cross-country hikes. While he enjoyed the intellectual vitality of New York City, he also yearned for the outdoor life. So he purchased an eighty-acre farm near Brewster, New York, and turned it into a rustic retreat.

On Friday afternoons he would drive up and spend the weekends away from the clamor of the city. Sometimes he would invite a few guests to go camping with him. There in the wooded wilderness of the Catskills they would meet another Dag Hammarskjold. Instead of the aloof, cultured diplomat, they met an outdoorsman in dungarees and dirty sneakers who was an expert at kindling a fire or identifying a hundred varieties of plant and bird life. In spite of his slim, almost frail build, Dag was in excellent physical condition. Gifted with the rugged stamina and toughness of the mountain climber, he seemed impervious to illness or cold or heat. A prodigious hiker, he would walk for miles at a relentless pace that wore out even the hardiest of his weekend guests. Therefore, while the UN post no longer left time for mountaineering, the Brewster retreat provided him with the next best thing—an opportunity to pitch a tent, chop wood, draw water and generally enjoy what he liked to refer to as "the strenuous life."

Even though Dag had few close friends, particularly among his UN colleagues, he was called upon occasionally to sponsor official receptions. These usually took place in the delegates lounge on the second floor. Smaller gatherings were held in his suite of offices on the thirty-eighth floor of the Secretariat Building.

His apartment on Park Avenue, however, was reserved for personal friends. When he did have guests at home they were usually artists, musicians or writers, including men like cellist Pablo Casals, composer Leonard Bernstein or author John Steinbeck. As a host he was urbane and informal, usually preferring to cook the meal himself and select the wines to go with it.

Because of the time-consuming nature of the Secretary-General's post, his social activities were severely limited. Moreover, his own desire for privacy and meditation caused him to turn down daily invitations to receptions and parties.

But in spite of his preference for solitude, he liked people. Reporters and others who knew him as unemotional and almost diffident were amazed to learn that he had an unfailing memory for the birthdays and anniversaries of friends, relatives and colleagues. On such occasions he never failed to send a card or a gift. "It's as if he has a calendar in his mind," an aide once confided to a surprised newspaperman.

The truth was that despite the aloof exterior, Dag was actually a deeply sentimental man. He could not stand suffering or distress in others. And news of the death of someone he knew even slightly made him morbid and despondent for days.

International tension, which had decreased following the release of the airmen and the success of the atomic energy conference in Geneva, boiled up again early in 1956. Suddenly —almost without warning, it seemed—the volatile Middle East rocketed into the center of the world scene for the second time in a decade. Actually, trouble had been brewing for some time, trouble which the rest of the world had conveniently tried to ignore in the ostrichlike hope that it would disappear if its existence were not recognized.

In truth, the UN had accomplished only a partial goal in stopping the war between the new state of Israel and the Arabs back in 1949. Having obtained a truce, it did nothing to follow up this success by concluding a permanent peace settlement. There were complex issues to be resolved, including the problem of what to do with hundreds of thousands of Arab refugees who fled Israel at the outbreak of the war and were now living in poverty in makeshift camps. And perhaps because of these difficulties the member nations of the UN found it easier to ignore the festering wound than to complete the task of healing it.

As the years went by, Arab-Israeli tension had increased. In 1954 Colonel Gamal Nasser seized power in Egypt and embarked on a campaign of hate and provocation in an attempt to stir up the Arab world against the Jewish state. *Fedayeen*— Arab commandos—crossed Israel's borders at night to attack settlements and destroy property. At the same time, the Soviet Union, set on exploiting the dispute, began to move into Middle Eastern affairs by supplying Egypt and other Arab nations with guns and planes.

Nasser, emboldened by Communist support, stepped up his anti-Israel campaign. At first the Israeli government appealed to the United Nations to stop the attacks, but when these pleas got nowhere she turned to a policy of reprisal. "We will deliver two blows for one," Premier David Ben-Gurion warned.

Teams of tough Israeli soldiers were sent across the border to attack Arab villages in retaliation for the *fedayeen* assaults. Snipers on both sides began to shoot across the border and succeeded in making these areas a virtual "no man's land." As a result of such incidents dozens of men, women and children as well as soldiers were killed and wounded. Clearly the dispute was plunging the Middle East headlong into another war.

The British and French, fearful for the safety of the Suez Canal—their lifeline in the Middle East—finally awoke to the danger. By announcing military preparations they hoped to warn the Israelis and the Arabs that they would intervene if war broke out. But their ally, the United States, was hesitant. Meanwhile the Russians, still intent on exploiting the issue, declared that military moves by the West would be considered a threat to the Soviet Union.

Dag was disturbed by the growing tension in the Middle East. Under the armistice of 1949 a United Nations Truce Supervisory Organization had been set up to see that the truce terms were observed. Through regular reports from the chief of the truce organization, a capable Canadian general named E. L. M. Burns, the Secretary-General was able to keep close tabs on developments. From Burns's dispatches it was clear that both Israel and the Arabs were in direct violation of the armistice provisions.

In January, Dag was scheduled to make a flight to Southeast Asia and Australia for routine talks. Why not stop off in the Middle East on the way? Accordingly, he made plans to visit Nasser and Ben-Gurion to find out at first hand what the dimensions of the problem were and what could be done to avert war.

Nasser listed a number of grievances. He charged that Israel was building fortifications in a "demilitarized" zone called El Auja. Premier Ben-Gurion, on the other hand, declared that Nasser had sent troops into El Auja, and that the Israelis, therefore, had acted to protect themselves from an Arab coalition that meant to destroy them.

By the time he returned to New York, Dag was convinced that formal discussion of the problems in the United Nations Security Council or the General Assembly would accomplish little except to aggravate suspicion and hostility. The situation was too complex and muddled to be settled by public debate. Besides, with the West and the Soviet Union at each other's throats there was little chance of getting them to back a specific course of action. No, this was a matter that could best be handled through "quiet diplomacy," he decided. By acting as a "middleman" in discreet behind-the-scenes negotiations, he might be able to accomplish what the public airing of charges and counter-charges on the floor of the UN could not.

The Secretary-General privately communicated his recommendation for secret negotiations to all the parties directly or indirectly concerned. The result was a resolution, introduced by the United States on March 20, asking the Security Council to direct the Secretary-General to look into ways of enforcing the Israeli-Arab Armistice provisions and "to arrange . . . any measure which . . . would reduce existing tensions. . . ." The Security Council approved the resolution.

Dag told the Security Council that he welcomed the mandate. But at the same time he implied that even if he had not been given the directive, he still could have acted under the provisions of the United Nations Charter. This was an important point, for above all he wanted to reaffirm for the future the right of a secretary-general to initiate independent action where world peace and security were threatened.

On April 6 Dag left for Beirut, capital of Lebanon, which was to be his headquarters while in the Middle East. During the next month he made a whirlwind tour of Egypt, Israel, Damascus and Amman. He met with Israeli and Arab spokesmen, including Ben-Gurion and Nasser. In the Israeli Premier's home, he drank lots of tea and argued for hours on end. The blunt-spoken Ben-Gurion, hostile at first, ended up admiring the penetrating mind and cultured tastes of the Swedish-born Secretary-General. In Cairo, Dag held long discussions with Nasser who appeared to be insecure about his own political position in the Arab world and indecisive in his diplomatic dealings.

Dag's goal in these private negotiations was to get hard-and-fast commitments from Ben-Gurion and Nasser to prevent further clashes along the border. What complicated his job was the curiosity of the press. Wherever he turned, dozens of reporters were there to fire relentless questions about the discussions and their progress. Side-stepping their inquiries was no easy task. A careless quotation in a newspaper or a statement published out of context would destroy the advances already made, hurting his further usefulness.

Through George Ivan Smith, his press representative, Dag replied to all questions with a vague "the matter is still fluid" or "there is flexibility in the situation." Such noncommittal statements did not satisfy the press and subjected the Secretary-General to criticism. But they prevented the negotiations from being wrecked by premature disclosures. To Dag that was the important issue rather than his personal popularity with the newsmen.

Finally, he managed to obtain commitments from both Arabs and Israelis to abide by the armistice provisions. As a result, a surprising change took place. A softer tone began to be heard in Jerusalem and Cairo, and the bloody border incidents grew less frequent. The mellowing attitudes of Ben-Gurion and Nasser were due almost entirely to the personal influence of Hammarskjold, who convinced each of his nonpartisan role and his dedication to finding a peaceful solution. As a middle man whose integrity and objectiveness could not be questioned by either side, he was thus able to get assurances from each to respect the cease-fire unconditionally, as long as the other party complied.

When Dag flew back to New York early in May, he could not help but feel that he had achieved more than he had dared to hope for. The Middle East controversy was stabilized for the time being. It was true that he had done nothing to solve such basic issues as the Arab refugee problem, issues that would have to be met in order to obtain a permanent settlement. But that had not been his goal. His immediate aim had been to prevent a deteriorating situation from disintegrating into war and to ease tensions. And this he had done. Now, perhaps, there *was* a basis for launching negotiations on the broader issues!

Dag's reasoning was simple. The cease-fire commitments had provided a psychological momentum for working out peaceful solutions. If the Security Council could be convinced of this fact, the way would be open for him to edge both sides toward the conference table. It would be tragic, indeed, if the impetus already achieved were now to be lost or ignored.

Dag's report on the results of his trip was submitted to the Security Council on May 9. Editorials called it a brilliant piece of work and hailed his diplomatic success with Ben-Gurion and Nasser as a major step forward toward peace in the Middle East.

The Security Council, too, praised Dag highly. "Mr. Hammarskjold's stature has been increased by the test to which we subjected him, and the same applies to the prestige—which I know to be dearer to him than his own prestige—of his office," declared Ambassador Herve Alphand of France to his fellow Council members.

In the weeks that followed, the cease-fire continued to hold. There were a few anxious moments when one side or the other raised charges of violations, but on the whole the border incidents remained at a minimum. The situation looked so promising that a resolution was introduced in the Security Council to provide a framework for negotiations on the more fundamental issues. But sharp disagreement between the Russians and the United States on procedures kept it from passing.

Dag was disconsolate at this failure—even though he had half anticipated such a turn of events—for he felt that the momentum for the settlement of basic problems had been dissipated. Nevertheless, in a statement to the press he held out the hope that the "legal cease-fire" eventually would be converted into "a state of mind."

But in July a series of events took place that completely altered the Middle East picture.

Chapter Thirteen

STORM OVER SUEZ

Since biblical days a narrow neck of land, stretching a hundred miles from the Mediterranean to the Red Sea, served as a gate-way between two worlds. For centuries it was one of the busiest and most important trade routes on earth. Here, across the hot desert sands of the Isthmus of Suez, early caravans first traveled between Asia and Africa, bringing to each the treasure and culture of the other.

Farsighted men had long dreamed of digging a "ditch" across Suez to establish an all-water route from the Western world to the Orient. Engineers said the project was impossible, but in 1859, through the efforts of Ferdinand de Lesseps, a de-termined French consul, a private company was formed to con-struct such a waterway.

Opened ten years later, the canal was only two hundred feet wide. This narrow trench across the desert was not at all impressive in appearance; yet it soon became one of the most important pieces of property on earth. By snaking through the one-hundred-and-four-mile stretch of canal, a ship could elimi-nate a six-thousand-mile trip down the coast of Africa and around the Cape of Good Hope!

The international importance of the canal was recognized in 1888 by a convention signed in Constantinople which guaran-teed the right of passage to all nations, in peace and war. Con-trolled by a governing board of members from several nations —majority stock was held by the French and British—the waterway was operated with scrupulous adherence to the provisions of the Constantinople Convention for more than sixty years.

For Great Britain, especially, the canal was a lifeline of empire. As a result, the British maintained strong military and naval bases in the Canal Zone to protect it against seizure and to guard against violations of the international agreement.

However, in the wake of the Israeli-Arab war in 1948–49 Egypt began to detain ships and seize cargoes bound to and from Israel. The matter was brought up before the UN. But in spite of Security Council protests to Egypt against these illegal acts, the practice continued. It constituted one of the major causes of friction between Israel and Egypt.

While Dag Hammarskjold was in the Middle East in April, 1956, trying to stave off a new Israeli-Arab war, other developments were under way. Egypt was involved in independent discussions with the United States to obtain funds to build a high dam at the town of Aswan on the Nile. Such help was tentatively promised by President Eisenhower, but on July 19 Secretary of State John Foster Dulles suddenly stated that his government was withdrawing its offer of aid.

Seething with anger, Nasser announced on July 26—just one week later—that Egypt was seizing the Suez Canal and would use the receipts from ships passing through the waterway to finance his dam. England and France wanted to dispatch troops and planes at once to force Nasser to relinquish control of the canal, but the United States, through Secretary Dulles, brought diplomatic pressure on its two Western Allies to keep them from using force. Britain and France finally relented, and the canal remained in Egyptian hands.

Dag viewed the situation realistically. The tensions created by the aggressive Egyptian move had all but made his successful cease-fire agreement a dead letter. Moreover, Israel saw in the seizure of the canal a direct threat to her own security. For Israeli spokesmen had expressed their fear that if Nasser's illegal acts were countenanced, he would grow bold enough to launch a full-scale attack against the tiny Jewish state.

On October 5 the Suez seizure issue was brought before the
Security Council and debated at open meetings. Simultaneously,
Dag tried to reconcile the controversy through behind-the-scenes
negotiations with the foreign ministers of Egypt, France and
Great Britain. He pointed out to them that as the UN representative his duty was to obtain a solution that would best
serve the world community as a whole. "Since world interest
and national interest are not wholly compatible, my task is to
help you reach agreements that will benefit your nations but
will also be consistent with the needs of the world community,"
he told them. Thus he hoped to set the groundwork for sincere
negotiation and compromise and to impress them with the importance of keeping the interests of the international community in mind at all times.

After six such meetings, general areas of agreement were
reached governing the principles under which the Suez Canal
should be operated. These were now incorporated into a resolution for consideration by the Security Council. A second part
was added to the statement, calling for international management of the Suez Canal by a board composed of the eighteen
nations that accounted for most of the tonnage passing through
the waterway.

The first portion of the resolution, dealing with general
principles of canal operation, was passed unanimously. The
second, outlining a specific plan of management, was vetoed by
the Soviet Union. Nevertheless, it was agreed that a valuable
starting point had been reached, and Dag was instructed to
continue with efforts to reach a negotiated full settlement of
the problem.

So satisfied was the Secretary-General with the progress made
that he proposed another series of private meetings. The British,
French and Egyptians agreed, and Dag made arrangements to
hold the negotiations in Geneva.

But on October 29 a bulletin clattered into the United Nations' teletype room which put an abrupt end to the negotiations. The Israeli army, the report said, had suddenly and ag-

gressively swept across the Egyptian-Israeli border and was knifing deep into the Sinai Peninsula!

As more details of the invasion poured in, it was obvious that this was no mere retaliatory raid but full-scale war. Sinai, the appendage stretching between Israel and the Suez Canal, belonged to Egypt. It was militarily significant as the base of operations for Nasser's *fedayeen* raids across Israel's border. Apparently, Ben-Gurion had grown tired of waiting for action against Egypt and had taken matters into his own hands. Superbly trained mechanized troops of the Israeli army sliced through the Egyptian regiments like a blade going through butter.

Dag was shaken to the core by news of the Israeli attack. True, Israel had been a victim of Arab provocation for months —years, in fact. Nevertheless, he couldn't help feeling that the United Nations had been betrayed by fate. He did not regret the loss of the months of effort that had gone into the negotiations with Ben-Gurion and Nasser as much as he feared that things were so far beyond control that the extension of hostilities was inevitable. Were all the slow, painful attempts to achieve a semblance of international order a waste of time after all? Was the United Nations itself doomed?

Dag suddenly awoke from his bitter reverie. He had been behaving like a fool, he decided. This was no time to lose faith or hope. If ever there was a need for clear thinking and determined action, this was it!

He was already making plans to call a meeting of the Security Council when he received a call from the United States delegation requesting that such a meeting be convened the next morning.

He met with Ambassador Lodge, who had been attending the opera and was still in white tie and tails, and together they planned strategy. It was agreed that the United States would introduce a cease-fire resolution to force Israel to call off her attack.

Dag stayed up all night preparing for the next day's meeting.

But when he showed up at the Security Council chamber in the morning, the delegates around the huge horseshoe table were amazed to find him clear-eyed, freshly shaved and impeccably groomed.

The debate on the United States resolution to secure a cease-fire lasted all day, but when the vote was taken, Britain and France registered vetoes! Dag was even more taken aback than the day before, when he had first received word of the Israeli invasion. At that particular moment, the huge mural on the wall of the Council chamber symbolizing man's quest for peace seemed a grim mockery.

After spending another sleepless night, Dag was in his seat when the Security Council reconvened the following morning. Dispatches from the Middle East now clarified the reasons for the Anglo-French veto of the cease-fire resolution. While the Israeli army was mopping up the remaining pockets of Egyptian resistance on the Sinai Peninsula, British and French planes were bombing Egypt's airfields as a prelude to sending in airborne troops to seize control of the Suez Canal!

In order to deal with the worsening crisis, a motion was introduced in the Security Council calling for an emergency session of the General Assembly. By sundown the following evening delegates from seventy-six nations convened in the huge domed Assembly Building. A resolution was presented by the United States calling for an immediate cease-fire and an embargo on the movement of troops and arms into the Middle East. It was adopted in the early morning hours by an overwhelming vote. The resolution also called for the restoration of freedom of navigation to the Suez Canal. And finally, it directed the Secretary-General to do all in his power to seek compliance with the provisions of the resolution.

Dag was well aware of the difficulties of the task assigned to him. It made the problem of seeking the release of the American fliers child's play by comparison. What if Israel declined to obey the cease-fire resolution? And suppose the British and French—whose invasion troops were already approaching the Egyptian coast—similarly refused? Dag reasoned that unless he could promise them that effective action to protect their interests would be taken, the attacking countries would ignore a call for a cease-fire.

He was right. Britain and France said they would comply with the resolution only if a UN force was sent to neutralize the area and prevent a recurrence of the incidents that had brought on the present situation. However, the Arab nations, backed by the Soviet Union, demanded that the UN restrict itself merely to restoring the *status quo,* as it existed before the Israeli invasion.

Dag pondered the dilemma carefully. Not the least of his problems was the lack of a United Nations police force. Even if the General Assembly did comply with the British-French demand for a UN force, where would it come from? How does one go about creating an army out of thin air?

As the crisis mounted, Britain and France stepped up their bombing operations against Egypt. Finally in the early morning hours of Sunday, November 4, the weary Assembly delegates passed a resolution directing the Secretary-General to prepare a plan for a United Nations emergency police force and report back within forty-eight hours! On the way out of the Assembly Hall, Dag told Dr. Ralph Bunche in a hoarse voice, "Now let us go and throw a police force together."

And that is exactly what they did.

Initially, Dag was skeptical about the possibility of creating such a force overnight. It would require the cooperation of many nations, cooperation that had not been forthcoming on the simplest issues. What hope was there that any country would now be willing to commit troops to such an unpromising venture as keeping peace in the strife-torn Middle East?

But in spite of personal doubts, Dag had been given a directive, one that he would do his best to carry out wholeheartedly. The tradition of civil service that had been instilled in him as a boy and had dominated his entire life would permit of nothing less.

For the next two days Dag and Ralph Bunche labored cease-
lessly to "throw a police force together." The Secretary-General
had almost no sleep at all for forty-eight hours, and Bunche
was equally fatigued. Yet a combination of physical stamina,
nervous energy and sheer determination kept them going. Except for a few minutes out to grab a hamburger and a cup of
coffee at an all-night luncheonette on Lexington Avenue near
UN headquarters, the Secretary-General and his aide worked
steadily hour after hour to blueprint a plan for a special force.

They called several delegations to sound them out on the
possibility of providing troops. The Scandinavian countries said
yes, tentatively. So did a few of the other small nations. Lester
Pearson of Canada offered to send a whole battalion, completely
equipped!

Dag also got in touch with the Colombian delegates. Yes,
they would be glad to ask their government for troops, and, yes,
there was a good possibility that the answer would be in the
affirmative.

By nine o'clock the following morning Dag had completed
the initial draft of the plan. After getting the reaction of several
delegates, he submitted it to the Assembly in the afternoon. The
blueprint called for the creation of a UN command with a small
staff of officers to supervise contingents of troops from various
nations. However, in order to divorce the operation from cold
war politics, it specified that no members of the special force
would be recruited from the big powers.

The report was approved 57–0, with nineteen countries ab-
staining. Thus, with little discussion and no fanfare, the United
Nations General Assembly had taken the unprecedented step
of creating the first genuinely international peace force in the
history of the world!

Now Dag and Bunche began to work on the second step of
their plan. Hurried calls to Washington brought together in
the Secretary-General's office the military attachés of all the
nations they had contacted earlier. The group met for hours on
end, hammering out the technical details of the proposed opera-

tion. The United States agreed to supply transportation through an airlift, although it was ruled out from providing officers and troops.

One of the most important features of the new police force was its UN command concept. During the Korean police action a unified command had been in charge. Made up of officers from several countries, it acted on behalf of the United Nations and conducted its operations under the blue and white UN flag. But it had not been under the authority of the General Assembly or the Security Council. Dag's plan, however, called for the UN command to be directly responsible to the organization itself; and it was this characteristic that gave it the unique distinction of being the first truly international force ever established by man.

Worn out though he was, the Secretary-General continued working at his desk until his eyes burned and he had to take a few minutes off to rest. Yet as the hours flew by he began to feel almost lighthearted. A major reason for this change in his spirits was the magnificent cooperation of the nations called in to help. Canada, Colombia, Denmark, Pakistan and Finland had agreed to supply troops. Norway, which had a law against sending contingents out of the country, had convened a special meeting of Parliament to approve an emergency bill giving the Cabinet the necessary authority.

Dog-tired but happy, Dag observed to an aide that "too often the criticism is made that the UN is letting the member nations down when, more often than not, the truth is that the nations of the world are letting the organization down. It has not been so in this case."

Egypt, its air force destroyed and its army battered, had earlier said it would abide by a cease-fire. On November 6 Israel joined Egypt and announced that it had halted its invasion and was accepting the UN cease-fire unconditionally.

Now there remained only Britain and France whose troops were driving toward the Suez Canal. Dag hurriedly completed his final report on the United Nations emergency force and rushed copies to the British and French delegations. Then he paced back and forth nervously chain-smoking his tiny ill-smelling cigars while he waited for an answer.

The British and French replies arrived in the afternoon. Dag immediately called a press conference. He told the reporters that he had an important statement to make. Then, after a short but dramatic pause, he declared in a tired but steady voice that Great Britain and France had ordered a cease-fire on the basis of the establishment of the UN police force. They had agreed to this action pending confirmation that Egypt and Israel had accepted the cease-fire unconditionally. "And I can confirm the cease-fire acceptance by the governments of Israel and Egypt," he added.

There was a mad scramble as the newsmen raced out of the room to get to their typewriters and telephones. A few minutes later, bulletins announcing the cease-fire were being transmitted by telegraph and radio to every corner of the globe.

On November 15 Dag boarded a plane at Idlewild Airport to fly to the Middle East to take personal charge of the launching of the police force operation. By the time he reached Egypt the first contingent of troops had already arrived. They wore blue arm bands to represent the United Nations, for there hadn't been time to have an official insignia made.

At Abu Suweir Airport, Dag, dressed in civilian garb, reviewed the troops after a brief talk in which he told them that they were taking part in a historic mission at a historic moment. He left the airport to attend the first in a series of conferences with the United Nations emergency force officers and Egyptian officials. There was a lot to be done. The Suez Canal had to be cleared of scuttled vessels, troops had to be stationed along the waterway and an orderly withdrawal of all foreign forces from Egypt had to be arranged.

In the next few days, Dag personally worked out many of the details and set a firm policy to be followed by the UN command. Even so, there was interminable negotiation with Egyptian officials, for it was one thing to establish policy and another to implement it in the light of the hundred and one unexpected problems that were bound to arise. Moreover, the Egyptians were extremely sensitive about their disastrous military showing, and sought to save face by imposing additional terms and conditions to indicate that they were victims rather than vanquished.

Dag also paid a quick visit to Israel to try to speed up the withdrawal of Israeli troops from the Sinai Peninsula. With William Ranallo, his bodyguard, and a small party he inspected UN border installations which were to serve as a buffer between the Arabs and Israelis.

In Jerusalem, a divided metropolis under the terms of the 1949 truce, the Secretary-General visited the Arab-controlled "Old City" and the "New City," which was the capital of Israel.

The inspection trip took place at high noon, under a broiling Middle East sun. The windless air enveloped the city like a shroud. Off to the east, beyond the Judean Plateau, Dag could see the valley of the Kidron where once the armies of King David had built their fortifications after Joab had wrested Jerusalem from the Canaanites.

As he strolled amid the ancient stone structures the Secretary-General recalled that here, just eight years before, another Swede named Count Folke Bernadotte had given his life in the cause of peace. Spotting a curious-looking lane, he and an aide began to follow the narrow path to see where it led.

They were some forty yards from the rest of the party when they heard the whine and the thud of a rifle bullet.

Dag whirled around. The shot, aimed by some unknown assassin, had whizzed past his ear, missing him by inches, then smashed into the wall behind.

"A bullet," said the aide in a tone of disbelief. "We're being shot at."

"Yes," Dag replied quickly. "Remember, we've seen or heard nothing. If this were to get out there would be another Arab-Israeli crisis."

They strolled swiftly back to rejoin the rest of the party. Dag smiled and called out in an even voice, "Gentlemen, let us leave here. It is too windy."

The others, sweating under the blanket of hot, motionless air, turned to stare at the Secretary-General as if he were mad. Then, spotting the wry grin on his face, they took his remark as a little joke and followed him to the waiting automobiles.

During the weeks that followed, the provisions of the cease-fire were carried out on a step-by-step basis, with Dag maintaining personal supervision of the over-all operation. Into his office in United Nations headquarters flowed daily reports on the progress of the emergency force's activities five thousand miles away.

By March, 1957—five months after the first Israeli units had invaded the Sinai Peninsula—the Secretary-General reported that all foreign troops had been withdrawn from Egyptian territory and that full compliance with the General Assembly's cease-fire directive had been achieved! The United Nations emergency force was now deployed all along the Egyptian-Israeli armistice line, he informed the Security Council.

Thus, while the basic dispute between Israel and the Arabs remained unresolved, the immediate crisis was over. War had been averted.

Chapter Fourteen

THE PATH OF A PEACEMAKER

Dag Hammarskjold was once asked what modern man needed most. He replied, "A firm faith in the capacity of men and governments to have the common sense to find their way out of the awful labyrinth of seemingly irreconcilable conflicts and insoluble problems in which we are now wandering."

While Dag's stunning success in Suez seemed to reflect a renewal of the "firm faith" he had prescribed, it was not an unadulterated triumph. At the same time that he was negotiating the historic Middle East cease-fire, other events were taking place that represented a tragic defeat for world order. In Hungary Soviet tanks were rumbling through the streets of Budapest in a brutal effort to crush the demands of the Hungarian people for freedom from Russian domination. The contradiction between the successful UN efforts to discourage aggression in the Suez and the blood being shed in Hungary was to give Dag nightmares for months to come.

The tangled web of circumstances leading up to the Hungarian massacre of 1956 had its beginning in World War II, when Hungary allied itself with Germany against Russia and the Western Allies. With the defeat of the Nazis, the country was occupied by Russia and a Communist regime was installed.

The dissatisfaction of the Hungarians with Soviet domination remained a potential powder keg for over a decade. In the fall of 1956 the people of Poland, also a Communist satellite, staged demonstrations to secure a greater measure of freedom from Russia—and succeeded. Encouraged by the events in

Poland and by radio broadcasts from private anti-Communist organizations abroad which implied that Western help would be forthcoming if a revolt were to occur, students in Hungary began to stage their own protests. They published a manifesto demanding sixteen reforms, including the withdrawal of Russian troops from Hungary at once.

The spark caught fire. By October 23 crowds of demonstrators were fighting the Hungarian Communist police in the streets and succeeded in capturing the Budapest radio station. The Hungarian government, in a state of panic, called Moscow for Soviet military assistance. The Russians complied by ordering their forces in Hungary to put down the uprising.

For three days fierce fighting took place between the Soviet troops, armed with tanks and cannon, and the Hungarian "Freedom Fighters" whose weapons were clubs, pickaxes and a few pistols and rifles. What had started out as a rebellion against the excesses of the Hungarian Communist government now turned into a fight for full independence from the Soviet Union. Hundreds of Hungarians and Russian soldiers were killed and wounded in the bloody conflict. But fists and rocks proved a poor defense against steel tanks, and by November 8 the fighting was over. The rebellion had been crushed in two weeks.

At the United Nations in New York a charge of Soviet aggression against Hungary was brought before the Security Council. A resolution calling on Russia to end her aggression was vetoed by the Soviet delegate. The matter was then referred to the General Assembly which passed a similar resolution on November 4 and instructed the Secretary-General to "investigate and report" on the charges against Russia. This was the same day that Dag had been asked to organize a UN police force for the Middle East!

Nevertheless, in spite of the crushing burden of work which kept him at his desk eighteen and twenty hours a day, he made a valiant effort to satisfy the demands that something be done about Hungary. On November 8 he asked Hungary to permit UN observers to enter the country to investigate and prepare a report. The request was abruptly refused. The Hungarian Communists, backed by the Soviets, claimed that the revolt and its suppression was an internal matter, and that since the Hungarian government had asked for Soviet help it did not constitute a legitimate issue for discussion under the UN Charter.

Dag was faced with a dilemma. Unable to gain entry into Hungary, he had to make an important choice. Should he devote most of his effort to the time-consuming job of negotiating with the Communists, or should he continue to give the bulk of his attention to Suez which held out a greater promise of success?

He chose the latter.

In the following months critics of the United Nations gleefully held up its failure in Hungary as proof of the organization's uselessness, ignoring altogether its success in Suez. The Secretary-General himself was attacked for "doing nothing" during the Hungarian revolt.

Dag was not concerned with the personal abuse heaped on him, but he did worry about the blow to UN prestige as a result of the Hungarian issue. In an attempt to set the matter straight, he explained in interviews and talks why nothing could be done. The United Nations, he declared, was not a world government. It was a parliament of nations, depending for its success on the willingness of each country to support its efforts. A major power, like the Soviet Union, could not be made to comply with a UN resolution unless the other nations were prepared to use force and thus precipitate a world war. In the Suez, however, the Israelis, British and French had been willing to submit to the *moral* force of the United Nations and the Secretary-General—something the Soviets had refused to do in the Hungarian situation.

"The crisis in Suez did not have a higher priority over that in Budapest because one was a more vicious form of aggression or a greater peace threat," Dag noted. "It was the accident of time and the way conditions fell together that dictated the choice. It was history itself, so to say, which arranged it that way."

In spite of everything, United Nations action on the Hungarian issue was not a total failure. In the months that followed, an investigation by a special UN committee under Dag heard more than a hundred witnesses who had fled Hungary, including government officials, journalists, engineers and student "Freedom Fighters." It also examined a mass of documents and other evidence bearing on the uprising and its suppression. The committee's report, issued in 1957, found that the events in Hungary "constituted a spontaneous national uprising." It charged that the Soviet Union, "in violation of the United Nations Charter, has deprived Hungary of its liberty . . . and the Hungarian people of the exercise of their fundamental rights."

The condemnation of Russian aggression was passed by the General Assembly, with negative votes cast only by the Communist countries. While it did not help the Hungarians directly, it was a distinct blow to Russian prestige. For millions abroad now recognized that Russian deeds were a far cry from her denials of aggressive intent.

In September of 1957 Dag came up for reappointment to a second five-year term as Secretary-General. The action of the Security Council was swift and decisive. The delegates delivered a series of glowing tributes to his past achievements, then voted unanimously to submit his name to the General Assembly.

The vote in the Assembly was also unanimous. The President described him as "surely our supreme international Civil Servant." He was lauded and applauded in the world press, even by some of those newspapers that had criticized him in the past.

Dag, however, looked upon his reappointment as more than an empty ritual. For four years he had tried to fulfill his commitment in the only way he knew how—with devotion, enthusiasm and an almost religious fervor. He could not help but feel, therefore, that his acceptance of a second term was really a rite of rededication—the act of renewing his vows. He had come a long way since that April morning in 1953 when he had stepped off the plane at Idlewild Airport. With the passing of time and events, he himself had grown and matured as an individual as well as an international statesman. He had become surer of himself, surer of the potential power of the United Nations.

True, some of his earlier ideals had faded. He knew now that the task of easing world tensions, particularly those between East and West, could not be done quickly. The problems of the world were too tangled to be unraveled overnight. For he realized what he had not seen so clearly before—indeed, it was the lesson Trygve Lie had tried to impress on him—that at a time of breaking and making of nations, of adherence to traditional and revolutionary new nationalisms and competing idealogies, there was no short cut to peace.

He saw, too, that the United Nations—an organization built out of the implements of an old world—could only carry out its tasks under the guiding spirit of a strong executive. Earlier he had agreed with Lie that a strong secretary-general was imperative; but he had seen it as the strength of a catalyst, an inspirer of action. By now he had discovered what his predecessor had learned before him—that the secretary-general must be more than an instrument or catalyst; *he must be a mover, a director behind the stage of international politics, but he must also be ready, where necessary, to step in and fill the role of actor in the world drama that was constantly unfolding.*

As secretary-general, Dag told himself, he had a prime responsibility for fashioning an international machine of world order in which the principle of peace would be "built in." Sometimes he demurred when people referred to him as a peacemaker. "Ultimately that is what I would like to be," he explained in his precise way. "But before we can have world peace, we must have world order. I am more like the artisan who builds a house brick by brick. Each new event, each new case that comes before us is a new brick in our house of nations. We use it as the foundation on which to place the next."

Initially, Dag had believed that the major concern of the UN was to find ways to eliminate the dangers of nuclear war. Now he realized that there was a second threat just as insidious— the small or "brush fire" wars. These were the outbreaks of violence that resulted from a world engulfed in nationalistic ferment, where small nations vented their hostility on their equally small neighbors. Since these were the conflicts that inevitably became entangled in big-power politics, anyone could serve as a spark to touch off nuclear war. The secretary-general, he felt, must serve as an international "fireman" to prevent the small conflagrations from starting and to help extinguish those that did flare up before they became "prairie fires."

Though Dag's concept of his job had changed, his basic faith in the future of the United Nations had not. If anything, it had been strengthened by his own personal involvement. He was convinced more than ever that the UN was the "last best hope of the world." But his idealism was firmly undergirded by an acceptance of the reality of world politics.

Ever since its inception the world organization had been tottering on the brink of invalidism, if not death. In every crisis that had arisen people had written it off. And yet it had managed not only to survive but to survive in strengthened form. There had been failure, and there had been success, and each success had provided a little more of that precious commodity —time.

Rereading the United Nations Charter, Dag was struck once more by the simple strength of that historic document. The brief preamble to the Charter said:

We the peoples of the United Nations, determined to save succeeding generations from the scourge of war which twice in our lifetime has brought untold sorrow to mankind, to reaffirm faith in fundamental human rights, in the dignity and worth of the human person, in the equal rights of men and women, and of nations large and small, to promote social progress and better standards of life in larger freedom, we have resolved to combine our efforts to accomplish these aims.

Dag could not help wishing that every human being in the world could read and understand those splendid words.

Early in 1958 the relative stability that had settled on the Middle East following the settlement of the Suez crisis threatened to disintegrate once again. But this time the issue centered around an internal struggle within the Arab world itself.

Despite a common language, religion and history, the Arab nations had long been torn by jealousies and hatreds. The world was surprised, therefore, when it learned on February 14, 1958, that the countries of Iraq and Jordan had merged to form a new Arab Federation. The reason for this sudden action was made clear a week later when Egypt and Syria announced that they were joining together to form a competing United Arab Republic—a move which apparently had been planned for some time. Thus Iraq and Jordan, strong rivals of Egypt, having learned of President Nasser's plans, had moved first to offset his anticipated action.

The fears of anti-Nasser Arabs were not without justification. For some time the Egyptian dictator had sought to become the rallying point for Arab nationalism throughout the Middle East and Africa. He envisioned himself as the leader of a new Arab empire similar to one that had once ruled from India to Spain. Countries like Iraq and Jordan, which hated Nasser, were afraid that their independence would be threatened by an Egyptian-Syrian merger. Therefore, by hastily forming their own coalition even before the announcement of the creation of the United Arab Republic, they hoped to strengthen their own hand against what was becoming known as "Nasserism."

The Egyptian leader attacked Iraq and Jordan as "stooges" of the Western imperialists and warned menacingly that "an accounting" was near. He predicted that his United Arab Republic would bring together all Arab countries "whether they like it or not, because it is the will of the Arab people on every spot of the Arab land." These were tough words, and their implications were not lost on the Arab countries. Throughout the Middle East, pan-Arab extremists took this as a signal to set in motion pro-Nasser demonstrations and propaganda.

One of Nasser's immediate targets was Lebanon, an advanced Arab country with a large Christian Arab population. The tension resulting from the Egyptian president's charges and demagoguery created jitters among the Lebanese leaders who feared an uprising among the Moslem Arabs within their borders. After heated debate, the government of Lebanon voted against alliance with either of the two Arab unions. It declared that "Lebanon shall remain a sovereign, independent, free and peaceful state, basing itself on the principles of the Charter of the United Nations. . . ."

The decision of the Lebanese to remain neutral set off a new wave of hysterical charges and propaganda by Nasser. Cairo Radio beamed denunciations of Lebanese officials and suggested that the government should be replaced. Nasser also denounced the United States and other Western influences on the Lebanese government. The verbal abuse and the emotional appeal to Arab nationalists had its effect. Antigovernment demonstrations were organized. When three Arab boys were sentenced to jail for tearing down and trampling a Lebanese flag, pro-Nasser activity was intensified.

By mid-April civil war threatened. Police were sent into the mountains in South Lebanon to hunt down rebel forces. In Tripoli, a Lebanese city, a pro-Nasser mob sacked and burned the United States Information Service library.

On May 12, armed insurrection broke out on the streets of Beirut, capital of the republic. Another USIS library was sacked and burned. At the same time, an automobile from Syria was stopped by Lebanese border guards because it seemed suspiciously heavy. A careful search revealed that it carried three submachine guns, twenty-eight pistols, fifteen hundred revolver bullets, fifteen thousand rounds of ammunition for other weapons, time bombs, demolition equipment and instruction sheets printed in Arabic on how to use the weapons and equipment!

Dr. Charles Malik, Foreign Minister of Lebanon, promptly accused the United Arab Republic of having incited and helped the rebellion against the government. He said, "We interpret this massive interference from outside as having everything to do with the events now unrolling in Lebanon." He cited a whole series of acts by the UAR, including at least sixty-two successful gun-smuggling trips by the automobile that had been stopped by the border guards, an attack by five hundred Syrians on a Lebanese customs station, and open incitement to Lebanese to riot by radio propagandists broadcasting from Egypt and Syria.

Two weeks later, on May 27, the United Nations Security Council met in New York to consider a complaint by Lebanon against the United Arab Republic for meddling in her internal affairs, "the continuance of which is likely to endanger the maintenance of international peace and security." Meanwhile, matters became even more complicated when John Foster Dulles announced that the United States was ready to land armed forces on the coast of Lebanon to prevent foreign attempts to overthrow the government!

Dag's view of the matter differed from that of the West. Embittered by Nasser's propaganda attacks and his direct interference in Lebanon, the United States and the Lebanese government had seen Nasser as *the* major villain of the new Middle East drama. The Secretary-General, however, could not help feeling that such an analysis was an oversimplification. Recalling his own impression of Nasser as a politician riddled with insecurity about his own position, Dag suspected that at least part of the reason for the Egyptian leader's aggressive acts stemmed from a deep-rooted, if unfounded, fear that the other Arab nations were plotting to overthrow him with the help of the West.

If this were the case, perhaps Nasser could be convinced to call a halt to his provocative behavior if he were assured that his suspicions were unfounded, Dag speculated. Certainly, approaching the problem in an initial spirit of negotiation was preferable to taking swift and extreme action against Egypt that might spark a new Middle East conflict with dire consequences for the whole world. Moreover, he was convinced that a strong resolution against Egypt would be vetoed by the Soviet Union, which had been supporting Nasser all along.

Accordingly, Dag drew up a careful plan of action. To bring it before the Security Council, he called in his old colleagues in the Swedish delegation and outlined his approach in a private conference. They endorsed his plan enthusiastically and agreed to sponsor a resolution.

In the meantime the press, unaware of his behind-the-scenes activity, demanded to know what the Secretary-General intended to do about peace in the Middle East.

"I have my dreams," Dag said.

"What are they?" a newspaper reporter wanted to know.

"I very rarely share my dreams with anybody," Dag replied wryly.

On June 11 a resolution introduced by Sweden was passed without a dissenting vote by the Security Council. It called on the Secretary-General to dispatch immediately a UN observer team to Lebanon to guarantee that there would be no illegal infiltration of personnel or arms or other material across Lebanon's borders.

At first many newspapers confused the observer team with a UN police force similar to that sent to Suez in 1956, but Dag set the issue straight. It was to be an "observer team" and not a police force at all, he stressed. The team's function would not involve military action but the halting of infiltration by spotting it and exposing it to world opinion.

While the United States and Lebanon were disappointed with what they regarded as "a weak resolution," they nevertheless decided to go along with it. Their support was due in large measure to their respect for Dag personally. They were convinced that if he favored the action it was worth giving it a try.

By June 16 almost half of a United Nations observer team that was to total a hundred military and diplomatic experts was already on the job in Lebanon, with observation equipment that included aircraft, helicopters and jeeps. Only five days had elapsed since the Security Council had passed the Swedish resolution!

Dag flew to the Middle East and quickly toured the various capitals, holding conferences with Arab leaders. Upon his return to New York, he reported to the Security Council that while there had been infiltration and attempts to stir up trouble from the outside, the Lebanese problem was fundamentally an internal one. "Only Lebanon can save Lebanon," he declared. The issue, he explained, was an extension of the more basic problem of Arab nationalism that would have to be solved by the various Arab states themselves, without interference by the West or the Communist world.

The United States was not happy with Dag's report. Secretary Dulles felt that the Secretary-General had not realistically appraised the danger of Egyptian propaganda attempts to stir up trouble among the Lebanese Moslems. He did not agree with Dag's sanguine conclusion that if encouraged to work out their problems among themselves the Arabs would arrive at a peaceful basis for coexistence.

Nevertheless, Dulles was prepared to leave matters in the hands of the United Nations for the time being. He even stated in a press conference that direct intervention should be avoided if the UN could do the job—a retreat from his previous announcement that the United States was prepared to move in troops to save the government of Lebanon.

Even a heat wave that swept over New York City in early July failed to wilt Dag's optimism as he continued to receive favorable reports from his observers in the field. Things were moving according to plan, as far as he was concerned. There was no reason to believe that this latest crisis would not be resolved peacefully, just as earlier problems in that troubled corner of the world had been settled by the UN in the past.

Chapter Fifteen

SPOKESMAN FOR WORLD ORDER

On July 14, a month after the creation of the United Nations observer team for Lebanon, the world was startled by news from Iraq, a partner with Jordan in the anti-Nasser Arab Federation. An army revolt had overthrown the government and its pro-Western leader, King Faisal, had been assassinated!

The telephones in Dag's office jangled constantly as diplomats called to find out what the news meant and to learn what the Secretary-General intended to do. Each caller was urged to be patient until the full implications of the situation were untangled.

Finally the telephone rang again. This time it was Secretary Dulles. In view of the Iraqi revolt the picture had changed, he told Dag. The United States was landing Marines in Lebanon— in response to an appeal from the Lebanese government—to help keep it from the same fate as the Iraqi government!

The following day, thirty-six hundred American marines in full battle dress, waded ashore at Beirut to the good-humored applause of hundreds of peaceful bathers and picnickers. There was no sign of revolt or violence of any kind, except for arguments between Lebanese soft drink vendors who elbowed each other out of the way in their eagerness to sell the perspiring marines Cokes and other American soft drinks.

Two days later Great Britain, taking its cue from the United States, landed two battalions of British paratroopers in Amman, Jordan, at the request of King Hussein who said he feared an "imminent attempt" by Nasser to overthrow his government!

Dag was dismayed by the decision of the United States and Britain to act so hastily. He knew only too well that it would set off international fireworks. Most of all, he feared that the impulsive gesture of landing troops would involve the Middle East in the cold war even more directly than in the past, the one thing he had been hoping to avoid.

As it turned out his worst fears were realized.

The Soviet Union immediately launched a scathing denunciation of the United States, accusing it of using "the big lie" and "the big cheat." The African and Asian nations uniformly attacked the Marine landings, and even some of the Lebanese officials, who had originally supported American intervention, now had second thoughts because of the unexpected sharpness of world criticism.

Even nations like Sweden, whose integrity was respected by the West, declared that the troop landings were not justified. In fact, except for grudging support by its European Allies and the pro-Western Arab states, the United States found itself under sharp attack by friends as well as enemies. It was an uncomfortable position to be in.

On August 8 an emergency special session of the General Assembly convened to deal with the Arab problem. Dag wanted to avoid at all costs a wide-open debate which he knew would deteriorate into charges and countercharges by the Soviet Union and the United States and accomplish nothing. So before the session opened he fell back again on his favorite tactic of laying a groundwork for negotiation by meeting secretly with a group of diplomats whose countries were not involved in the crisis. He pointed out that elections held the week before in Lebanon had brought a new president into power who had already secured the support of Christians and Moslems. Under these circumstances, the Secretary-General declared, the time seemed ripe for serious negotiation on the Arab issue.

What specifically did he propose? someone asked. A long-range program Dag replied. He wanted to continue the observer team in Lebanon. He wanted the Arab states to reaffirm the principle of nonaggression and to undertake conciliatory talks with the help of the United Nations. He also wanted the East and the West to pledge a "hands-off" policy so the Arabs could settle their own problems without big-power interference. And finally he wanted the Arab countries to launch a cooperative regional economic development program—with UN support and technical assistance—that would help not only individual countries but the Middle East as a whole.

How did the Secretary-General intend to present his program? Dag told the diplomats that he would try to get the floor of the Assembly as soon as the meeting was called to order. In that way East-West debate and wrangling would be headed off from the start. Then he would need their help in convincing other member nations to support his proposals.

By the time the Assembly session opened, word had spread of Dag's plan and therefore many of the member delegates were prepared for the sequence of events that was about to take place. The Assembly President, Sir Leslie Munro of New Zealand, banged down his gavel calling the session to order, and paid tribute to the "distinguished Secretary-General and his able staff." Then Dag took the floor and outlined his approach. Delegate Sobolev of the Soviet Union got up to attack the United States, but the attack was far milder in tone than had been anticipated. Now U.S. delegate Lodge got up and, after going through the ritual of denying the Soviet charges, suggested that the members of the Assembly not waste their time with senseless recrimination which would add nothing to solving the problem. This, too, represented a surprising change from the American position of previous weeks!

When the thirty-five-minute session came to an end, Dag was delighted with the way things had gone. Even the tone of debate seemed to have been transmuted from anger and insult to calmness and reason on all sides.

With his plan of action off to a good start, Dag now went to work to implement it. In his thirty-eighth floor office he went through the now familiar process of talking privately with key delegates, trying to convince them to go along with his proposals. And in the delegates lounge, his neutral "allies" like Sweden, Norway and Denmark lobbied among the other nations to support the Secretary-General's approach.

The quiet behind-doors campaign worked beautifully. Now that the heat and emotionalism had worn off, the big powers were in a mood to listen more attentively and objectively than before. Gradually, pressures built up among the smaller powers for a resolution that would incorporate Dag's proposals.

In the following days a number of resolutions were brought before the General Assembly and debated. Then, on August 20, the delegates of ten Arab nations, after meeting privately at a Manhattan hotel, circulated a resolution of their own, reflecting almost exactly the Secretary-General's ideas as he had outlined them at the opening of the special session.

The delegates to the General Assembly were amazed at this show of Arab cooperation by countries who only a short time before had been attacking one another and charging each other with aggression. The following day the Arab proposal was adopted unanimously by the Assembly. It became known as the "Good Neighbor Resolution."

Privately Dag exulted. He knew, of course, that the passage of the resolution would not work miracles. There was still a long way to go before the Arabs surmounted their national animosities and got down to applying in a practical way the general principles of a "good neighbor" policy. But a philosophy had been set, one designed in the long run to bring greater peace and stability to the turbulent Middle East. Even more important, the world had once again been snatched away from the brink of war through timely action within the UN.

The day after the Good Neighbor Resolution was passed, Dag permitted himself a rare bit of public boasting. He told the press that the day before had been "one of those days in the life of this organization when it showed its invaluable contribution to present politics in the international field and to present diplomacy."

On August 25 Dag flew to the Middle East to see that the initial provisions of the General Assembly resolution would be carried out. Two weeks later, the United States announced that it was withdrawing an initial contingent of seventeen hundred marines from Lebanon and shipping them back to the United States because they were no longer needed!

It was not often that Dag found time for quiet reflection these days. Except for a rare stolen weekend when he journeyed up to Brewster, his main source of relaxation was reading. In addition to the works of prose writers, he read and translated foreign poetry into Swedish. Even as a child the art of the poet had held a fascination for him which he never outgrew. After a twelve- or fourteen-hour stint in his office, he found nothing quite as soothing as a book of French poetry while a hi-fi recording of Bach's *Fifth Brandenburg Concerto* played in the background.

Although Dag considered his own talents as a poet meager, he got a vicarious satisfaction from translating the works of others. He was already in the process of completing a translation into Swedish of some of the works of the contemporary French poet, St.-John Perse. And eventually, he hoped to do the same for some of the essays of Martin Buber—provided he could ever find the time.

But except for his poetry and his weekends at Brewster, life for the Secretary-General continued to be a furious round of work and travel. By now his journeys had taken him to virtually every member nation of the UN, and he had flown so many hundreds of thousands of miles that he could not even begin to estimate the distance.

Yet on the few occasions when he did find the time to indulge himself in the luxury of self-probing, he felt a vague sense of discontent, frustration even. In spite of the triumphs of the past six years, he could not help feeling that in one respect he had failed. When he had taken the job of secretary-general in 1953 he had done so with the high hope of helping to ease the cold war—the basic stumbling block to a real and lasting peace. In this he had not succeeded. Despite occasional and limited moments of international calm, the principle of world order was still struggling to extricate itself from the vise-like grip of the East-West deadlock.

True, the possession of atomic arms by both sides had created a balance of nuclear terror that seemed to rule out the deliberate use of such weapons by the big powers. But this had not eliminated the small brush fire war with its potential for accidentally engulfing the whole world in a nuclear holocaust.

The real question was how long the people of the world would continue to endure the tensions of a cold war without losing faith in the ideal of international order. From the start the United Nations had had its enemies. There were those in the West who contended the UN was a scheme to allow communism to gain control of the world. And in the Communist nations there were fanatics who claimed the world organization was a capitalistic device controlled by reactionary imperialists intent on destroying communism.

Finally, there were the visionaries who had dreamed that with the creation of the United Nations the lion and the lamb would automatically lie down together. And such idealists, too, constituted a danger, Dag felt. There was nothing wrong with idealism provided the idealist did not allow himself to become starry-eyed and kept his feet planted firmly on the ground. Idealism, when not tempered with reality, could lead to cynicism and bitterness. What was cynicism after all but idealism turned sour? The cynic who had lost his faith in the United Nations could prove to be the real instrument of its destruction, just as those who had lost faith once before had succeeded in destroying the League of Nations, Dag told himself.

He had always felt that the supreme challenge of the United Nations was the settlement of the conflict between communism and the West. His experience of the past six years had strengthened this conviction. For in spite of all that had transpired—in spite of the temporary victories and the momentary ebbing of tensions—the resolution of the basic cold war issues still seemed as remote as ever; so remote that he had long since stopped dreaming of a single over-all settlement and now contented himself with the hope of a piecemeal resolution of issues over a long period of time. The most that could be achieved in the foreseeable future, he concluded, was a tolerable form of peaceful coexistence. It was the United Nations' task to act as a "center of reconciliation" in order to gain the precious time necessary to usher in a period of peaceful coexistence and, eventually, a legitimate negotiated settlement of all major international issues.

Dag missed no opportunity to preach this gospel to both the East and the West. With the Russians, however, he had started out with the added disadvantage of trying to overcome their inherent suspicion of anyone from a non-Communist nation. However, as the years passed, many of the Communist diplomats —like the delegates from the West—had learned to trust and respect him. Seated in his office on the thirty-eighth floor he was a repository of top-secret confidences, not only from the Western diplomats but from the Soviet and satellite representatives as well.

There were occasions, of course, when diplomats on both sides differed strenuously with his conclusions and approach. Occasionally these disagreements were so vigorous that it approached irritation and mutual resentment. But on one point everyone—Communist and non-Communist—agreed: once Dag was told something in confidence, his discretion and ability to keep a secret was beyond question. It was one of the most important reasons for his effectiveness in establishing the United Nations as a "center of reconciliation" during the multitude of international crises that constantly arose.

Early in 1959 Dag was invited to fly to Russia to meet with Premier Nikita Khrushchev. The Secretary-General was delighted. He saw it as an ideal opportunity to convince the Soviet leader of the importance of placing greater reliance on the UN for the settlement of disputes. He knew that within the Russian Foreign Ministry, as in the foreign offices of other nations, there was a sharp split between officials who were willing to utilize the UN and those who distrusted its chances of success in solving major problems and wanted to use it only as a platform for propaganda.

In March he flew to Sochi, a magnificent resort on the Black Sea. There he met the squat, bald-headed Soviet premier who promptly invited him to go rowing! With the powerfully built Khrushchev straining at the oars and boasting that he could row for miles without tiring, the tiny boat bobbed its way over the gentle waves.

They debated at great length about the United Nations. Dag listened attentively to the Communist premier's complaints that the organization was dominated by capitalists and imperialists, then tried to rebut his host's arguments. Later that night there was a magnificent dinner.

Among the other guests at the dinner were Russia's leading foreign officials, including Ambassador Andrei Gromyko. Pointing at the dour Gromyko with a stubby thumb, Khrushchev grinned and told Dag, "If I had listened to that fellow Gromyko, you would not be here now. He thinks you're a Western agent and should not be permitted in the Soviet Union."

Another Soviet official, Anastas Mikoyan, explained good-naturedly that in Marxist philosophy there was no such thing as an individual who is neutral and objective. "Everyone is an agent, even if he's from Sweden," Mikoyan said jokingly.

Dag put down his glass slowly. "As Secretary-General of the United Nations, I am, in one important respect, like your own famous Sputnik," he replied to Khrushchev with a wry smile. "True, I was launched in Sweden, but once in orbit I do not come close to any country."

Chapter Sixteen

DRUMS ALONG THE CONGO

On a grander scale than ever before, the post-World War II era was swept by forces expressing the fierce determination of men to be free. This liberating force was felt particularly in the colonial empires which the nations of Europe had created in Africa and Asia centuries before.

In the fifteen years after the end of the war, new nations representing over a billion people emerged from colonial status and entered the family of independent states. By 1960 the United Nations increased its membership from fifty-one nations to more than seventy. Without question, the age of imperialism was in its twilight.

Dag Hammarskjold saw in the demise of the great colonial empires grave international problems as well as bold new challenges and opportunities. To the new countries emerging from foreign domination, the existence of the United Nations was of vital importance. It represented a "third force" which could protect them from future imperialism. Through its special agencies, it was also a source of desperately needed assistance in the economic and social spheres.

The colonial system, whatever its defects, had kept peace and order in the colonies and had helped them develop material resources. Some of the more enlightened powers, like England, had trained native leaders and technicians and even implanted democratic political and social institutions.

With the disintegration of colonialism, a vacuum was created. Some nations, like India, had been prepared for freedom.

Their native leaders immediately moved in to take over the reins of government from their former rulers. In such cases, the transition proved to be orderly and relatively painless.

But many colonies had not been educated for independence. This was particularly true in Africa where some of the most ruthless colonial exploitation had taken place. There, many of the former colonies caught up in the surge toward national freedom were pitifully unequipped to cope with their new independence.

While many statesmen and diplomats in the large nations were unaware of the restless stirrings on the Dark Continent, Dag had been concerned with it almost from the moment he took office. One of his key aides, Heinrich A. Wieschhoff, had been selected especially because of his expert knowledge of Africa. Until then, the African problem had received a low priority on the roster of issues with which the UN Secretariat occupied itself.

With the admission of nearly twenty new African states to the United Nations, and others due to become independent soon, Dag decided early in 1960 to take a firsthand look at Africa.

With a small party of aides, including Wieschhoff, he set out on a six-week tour of what was once a vast colonial preserve. Flying from capital to capital, they toured mines and factories, met with government leaders and discussed the gamut of social and economic problems faced by these new states.

Everywhere Dag saw signs of political and nationalistic upheaval. There were dangers to be sure—dangers of economic crisis, political opportunism, inept leadership. There were insufficient people trained for government work, inadequate schools, lack of technicians to develop economic resources. Moreover, many of the African peoples were so embittered by colonial exploitation that their political outlook was dominated by an extreme form of nationalism based on hatred of Europeans.

But Africa spelled opportunity, too, Dag sensed—a chance for the United Nations to demonstrate, as never before, its potential for helping struggling new countries and developing loyalties to the concept of a world community. However, achieving this goal would mean keeping Africa from becoming embroiled in cold war politics, providing vast amounts of technical help, offering assistance and counsel to the inexperienced leaders of these new governments. A large order? Perhaps. Yet Dag was convinced it *could* be done. It *had* to be done, if that vast, mysterious world south of the great Sahara were to be kept from becoming another powder keg of potential conflict like the simmering Middle East.

On his return to United Nations headquarters, Dag went to work at once on a major plan for African development. The heart of his proposal called for a series of economic and technical aid programs to new African states that would provide the UN with an opportunity to establish a network of Secretariat teams throughout Africa. These experts would help ease the transition between colonialism and independence and keep the emerging states free of East-West politics.

But before he could complete his blueprint, an event took place that thrust the green hills and sun-drenched plains of Central Africa squarely into the middle of the world stage.

The curtain was raised on this latest international drama on June 30, 1960. On that day the Belgian Congo secured its independence from Belgium and became the Republic of the Congo. In less than a week, the new Congo nation became a seething cauldron in which the troubles of a century suddenly boiled over, with tragic consequences for Africa and the world.

Ever since 1885, when King Leopold of Belgium had taken over the Congo as a private preserve of the royal family, native resentment had been building up. By 1908, abuses in the territory had stirred world opinion to such an extent that Belgium was forced to annex the Congo as a colonial possession and institute minimum reforms.

But in the half century that followed, the Belgian government did nothing to prepare the Congo for eventual independence. Then, bowing to the irresistible urge of native nationalism, Belgium called a conference of native leaders early in 1960 and agreed on a plan for Congolese freedom to be implemented in six months.

The plan was simple enough: once an "independent" government was set up, Belgium would continue to administer the country from behind the scenes. The Belgian strategists had good reason to believe the tactic would work. In a population of thirteen and a half million and an area of nine million square miles—a territory one third the size of the United States— there were only sixteen Congolese who had been graduated from a college or university! There were no native doctors, lawyers or engineers. Even the twenty-five-thousand-man Congolese army had no Congolese officers. Moreover, in Katanga Province, where the Congo's mineral and industrial wealth was concentrated, the mines and factories were operated by a giant corporation known as the Union Minière, an enterprise controlled by Belgians.

In theory, Belgium's strategy to retain control of the Congo was sound. But it failed completely to take into account the strength of African nationalism and the bitter anti-Belgian feelings of the Congolese built up over a century of exploitation.

Less than twenty-four hours after the Congo became an independent nation, it began to fall apart in civil warfare. Dag first learned of the tragedy that was about to unfold when a series of ominous cables arrived from Ralph Bunche who had flown to Léopoldville, the Congolese capital, to represent the United Nations at the Independence Day ceremonies on June 30. Bunche informed him that fighting had broken out between rival tribes. Furthermore, the army, no longer under Belgian control, had mutinied against their inexperienced native officers and gone on a bloody rampage of killing and looting.

Within a week, Belgium announced that she was sending paratroopers back to the Congo to restore order. A day later Moise Tshombe, pro-Belgian leader of rich Katanga Province, announced that Katanga was seceding from the Congo—a violation of the Congolese independence agreement. Moreover, with the help of the wealthy Union Minière mining combine he began to recruit white mercenaries to lead his Katanganese army.

Dag, in constant touch with Bunche, decided that the United Nations could best help by dispatching a force of experienced officers and noncommissioned personnel to bring the Central Congolese army under control, instill it with a sense of discipline and train a corps of native officers.

But before the plan could be carried out, an urgent cable reached Dag's desk from President Joseph Kasavubu and Prime Minister Patrice Lumumba of the Congolese government. It was a desperate appeal to send United Nations troops at once to protect the Congo from outside aggression. Kasavubu and Lumumba charged that Belgium had committed an aggressive act in sending paratroopers back to the Congo, and accused her of instigating Katanga's secession from the central government.

For Dag this was a predicament. No formal request had gone to the Security Council to take up the question, either from the Congo government or from a member of the Council. Would he be wise in bringing the issue before the Council on his own?

This was a question that went to the very heart of the role of the Secretary-General. The Congo issue was a touchy one. If he were to act on the plea of the newborn African state, he would antagonize Belgium and possibly other colonial powers like England or France.

On the other hand, if he played it safe and cabled Kasavubu and Lumumba that an official request would have to go to the Security Council itself, precious time would be lost.

He weighed the question carefully. The overriding consideration at the moment, he felt, was to keep the Congo problem free of big-power politics. The presence of Belgian troops in the country was the opening wedge. It provided an excuse for the Soviet Union to become involved. Already there were alarming reports that the Russians were beginning to pour political advisers, "technicians" and military supplies into the area. Once the Communists secured a foothold, the United States and Britain would have to act to protect Western interests. The result would be chaos, with the Congo serving as a battlefield in the cold war.

He recalled what had happened in Spain a quarter of a century before. The League of Nations had not acted to keep Fascist and Communist forces out of the Spanish Civil War, and as a result Spain had become a bloody preamble to a world war. The failure of the League in that instance had been one of the primary causes of its demise. Was history about to repeat itself?

On the afternoon of July 13, Dag made a solemn decision. He sent out a call for the Security Council to meet that evening on the Congo question, invoking the right of the secretary-general, under Article 99 of the United Nations Charter, to take action when there was a threat to international peace and security. It was a fateful moment. Only once before in United Nations history had this authority been used—when Trygve Lie had called a meeting of the Security Council in order to initiate the police action in Korea. Because of it, Lie had antagonized the Soviet Union and brought about his own downfall.

Dag was well aware of the dangerous ground he was on, but he had searched his own conscience and was convinced it was the only honorable course to take. More than his own future hung in the balance—the future of the United Nations itself.

At 8:45 P.M. the Security Council convened. Dag took the floor and outlined the Congo crisis. He argued that the presence of Belgian troops in the African state had created international tension and was unacceptable as a method of preserving peace and maintaining order.

"I strongly recommend," he stated, "that the Council authorize the secretary-general to take the necessary steps, in consultation with the government of the Congo, to provide the government with military assistance during the period which may have to pass before, through the efforts of the government with technical assistance of the United Nations, the national security forces are able to fully meet their tasks. It would be understood that were the United Nations to act as proposed, the Belgian government would see its way to a withdrawal."

In the hours that followed, the Soviet and United States delegates attacked each other bitterly. Russia's Arkady Sobolev accused the United States of "direct participation in the conspiracy of the colonizers against the young Republic of the Congo." He charged that the Western powers intended to intervene in the Congo.

He also attacked Dag for allegedly exceeding his powers in calling the meeting in the first place. But when Dag rebutted him sharply by citing the authority given the secretary-general under the UN Charter, the Russian delegate decided not to press the issue. Then U.S. delegate Lodge attacked Sobolev for engaging in "a ponderous, long-winded bit of Communist nonsense."

And so it went into the early morning hours. . . .

At 3:00 A.M. a resolution was introduced by Tunisia encompassing Dag's proposal. It was passed immediately by the Council members with abstentions by France, Nationalist China and the United Kingdom. Amazingly enough, in spite of the earlier rancor, the United States and the Soviet Union had seen eye to eye on the action to be taken! Thus once again a UN peace force had been created to stamp out a brush fire before it could spread into a world-wide conflagration.

Within forty-eight hours after the passage of the resolution, the first United Nations contingent landed at Ndjili airport in Léopoldville. By the end of the week there were thirty-five hundred troops, including Ethiopians, Ghanians, Moroccans and Tunisians. With each passing day the United Nations force in the Congo grew in strength, drawing its support from the smaller neutral nations. This followed the principle laid down by Dag that the peace action should be kept absolutely free of entanglement in big-power politics. Almost immediately Belgium began the withdrawal of her occupation troops. And some weeks later, the Central Congolese army, backed by the presence of United Nations troops, expelled the large number of Communist agents sent in by the Soviet Union.

With the danger of intervention from the outside checked, Dag felt that an important victory had been won. But his troubles were not yet over. What was now taking place was a confusing conflict within the Congolese government itself that is probably unmatched in modern history.

It took the form of a struggle for power between President Kasavubu, a moderate, and Prime Minister Lumumba, a leftist. The political tangle was further complicated by the refusal of Katanga to end her secession. Finally, after months of wrangling, Lumumba was kidnaped by political enemies and taken to Katanga where he was murdered, allegedly in the presence of Katanganese government officials.

As the weeks passed, a number of attempts at Congo unity were made, but they all ended in failure, mainly because of Tshombe's refusal to allow his secessionist province to join the central government. One of the key roadblocks was the presence in the Katanganese government and army of hundreds of Belgian and other foreign mercenaries. Backed by the Union Minière, they did everything in their power to prevent an accord on Congo unification.

Nevertheless, Dag continued to urge the central Congolese government to try to reach a peaceful agreement with Katanga. The Russians demanded that he use United Nations troops to force Katanga to end its secession, but Dag refused. He was convinced that until all possibilities of negotiation with Tshombe were exhausted, the use of UN troops to achieve a political settlement would be unwise and dangerous. It would merely prolong bitterness and dissension for years to come and might even rend the newborn state asunder in civil war. Dag's firm position thus set him squarely at odds with the Soviet Union.

With the opening of the Fifteenth General Assembly of the United Nations on September 20, 1960, the issue was brought to a dramatic climax.

Chapter Seventeen

THE SOVIET CHALLENGE

Almost two months before the General Assembly meeting, Premier Nikita Khrushchev had called for the heads of the member nations to take part personally in the coming sessions in New York. President Eisenhower and the other Western leaders were apprehensive. East-West relations had been at a low ebb for weeks because of the Congo crisis and other disputes. Therefore, the sudden proposal by the Communist leader was viewed with cynicism. It was clear that what Khrushchev was seeking was not a meeting of minds but a world-wide propaganda forum.

Dag shared this apprehension. He felt that because of the recent international difficulties a sudden "summit meeting" of the heads of state, without preliminary meetings at the lower diplomatic levels, could do incalculable mischief; that instead of easing, it would harden the already serious tensions.

Khrushchev, however, plunged right ahead. He announced that he was coming to New York as head of the Soviet delegation to the Assembly. The heads of the satellite Communist states, having received their cue, declared that they would attend, too.

Now the stampede was on. One by one the leaders of the neutralist nations indicated their intention to show up. And in the face of these developments, the leaders of the West found themselves in an embarrassing corner. Reluctantly they agreed to be present when the Assembly opened.

Even before Khrushchev's white ship, the *Baltika,* entered New York Harbor, the tone of the forthcoming session was set when a Soviet official delivered a vicious attack on Dag as a "stooge" of the colonialists. The Secretary-General did not reply to this assault, but he knew that it was a storm signal of trouble to come.

Hundreds of thousands of New Yorkers excitedly crowded the sidewalks and streets to catch a glimpse of the heads of every important nation in the world as they converged on Manhattan's East Side for the General Assembly meeting.

The opening sessions were turned into a crude political circus. Khrushchev interrupted the proceedings rudely, referred to other delegates in unflattering terms and heckled the speakers unmercifully. On the sidewalks outside, the atmosphere in the Assembly Hall was matched by demonstrators of every political hue, who pushed and shoved and shouted, in spite of the efforts of the New York police to maintain order.

On the third day of the meetings Dwight D. Eisenhower delivered a speech backing Dag's efforts to bring peace to the Congo. He criticized the "few nations" which wanted to prolong friction in that troubled part of Africa for their own purposes. To the United Nations membership he proposed a pledge of noninterference in the internal affairs of African states and a suggestion that economic and educational aid be given Africa to strengthen the development of the new nations. Warm applause greeted his statement of principles.

The next day Premier Khrushchev got to his feet to address the Assembly. In tone it was the direct opposite of Eisenhower's talk. The chunky bald-headed Communist leader shook his fist angrily as he proceeded to deliver a bitter tirade against the United States. The time had come for the remaining colonial areas to revolt against the West, he shouted. Following this theme, he proceeded to accuse the Western nations of a series of international crimes probably unmatched in history. The diatribe lasted for two hours!

Then, after having tired of hurling invectives at the "Western imperialists," he turned to his real target—Dag. As the Assembly listened in shocked amazement, the Soviet head accused the

Secretary-General of siding with the colonialists in the Congo and of having improperly used the UN force against the interests of the Africans!

Seated below the great seal of the United Nations, Dag listened with seeming impassiveness to this frenzied attack on his integrity and competence. Occasionally his brow furrowed and his arm trembled as he held two fingers against the side of his forehead in a characteristic gesture of intense concentration. But he continued to stare straight ahead, without even a glance at the speaker.

The tirade continued. Finally, Premier Khrushchev, after having traveled a circuitous verbal route, came at last to the true reason for his speech. Indeed, observers later concluded that it had been the main purpose of his coming to the General Assembly meeting in the first place.

His government, Khrushchev declared blandly, had decided that the office of secretary-general "who alone governs the staff and alone interprets and executes the decisions of the Security Council and sessions of the UN General Assembly should be abolished."

In the deadly silence that followed, the Communist leader proceeded to outline a plan for an executive body of three which would represent the three political forces in the world: "the Western powers, the Socialist states and the neutralist countries." This group would replace the present post of secretary-general! Khrushchev stated triumphantly.

Almost as abruptly as he had begun his attack, the Russian premier ended his speech, turned to glance at Dag and grinned broadly. Then he removed his spectacles and strode with comic jauntiness to his seat, while the Communist bloc applauded wildly. At that point, Assembly President Frederick Boland of Ireland adjourned the session.

Over the weekend the Western diplomats huddled together in perplexed gloom as they struggled to find a way to reply effectively to the assault of the Soviet leader. At the same time Khrushchev, smug and satisfied, used the intermission in the world drama to expound further on his proposal for a three-man body to replace Dag. To newspapermen he stated with the force of an ultimatum that unless a reorganization took place to provide for political representation in the Secretariat, there could be no solution to the disarmament problem and other vital issues.

Secluded in his Park Avenue apartment, Dag used the weekend for morbid self-searching. Khrushchev's carefully contrived attack was more than the wild outburst it seemed. The Secretary-General's integrity had been impugned, and he had been subjected to malicious personal abuse. To all intents and purposes, his effectiveness as a middleman had been undermined if not destroyed, for it seemed certain that the Soviets were saying they would no longer work with him.

Dag could not help wondering at the grim irony of things. Here, seven years later, he found himself in the same dilemma as his predecessor Trygve Lie, and for the same reason—defending the integrity of the secretary-general's office. Yet they had arrived at the identical point through different routes. Lie, the bluff, colorful extrovert, had been pilloried by the Russians for his outspokenness and his independence during the Korean crisis. Dag, who had desperately sought to avoid Lie's errors by wearing the mask of the colorless bureaucrat while pursuing a policy of "quiet diplomacy," was now being attacked for his independence in handling the Congo issue. History played strange tricks, the Secretary-General mused.

Once Lie had been convinced that his usefulness was at an end, he had resigned. Shouldn't he do the same thing? Dag asked himself. Would it not be better to remove himself as an object of controversy at this time so that the United Nations could get on with its work? But as the weekend wore on he was torn by a nagging sense of guilt. Resigning now would be too easy. It would be the coward's way out. The issue was not the Russian attack on Dag Hammarskjold, the individual. Far more fundamental was the threat to the basic concept of an independent Secretariat.

The Communists were attacking the very existence of a secretary-general's office which would have no commitments to any nation or group of nations, or to any political ideology save that of the principle of international order and peace. Thus they were out to destroy the very keystone of the United Nations, and it was the continued existence of world organization that was at stake.

If the UN was still an imperfect international instrument, it was so because it symbolized the imperfections of an imperfect world, Dag reflected solemnly. Still, imperfect as it was, it was the only salvation left. And only the fact that it existed at all held out the promise of bettering the lot of mankind as humanity struggled up the steep path toward international understanding.

The atmosphere in the domed hall was heavily charged with suspense when the General Assembly resumed its meeting on Monday morning. As soon as the session was called to order, Dag got the floor. He began his reply to Khrushchev in a high-pitched but unemotional voice.

The issue raised by the chief delegate from the Soviet Union, he began, was fundamental to the concept of the United Nations. It was not the man but the institution that was of moment. . . .

The delegates from seventy countries leaned forward in their seats anxiously as the Secretary-General declared, "Use whatever words you like—independence, impartiality, objectivity—they all describe essential aspects of what, without exception, must be the attitude of the Secretary-General.

"Such an attitude may at any stage become an obstacle for those who work for certain political aims which would be better achieved if the Secretary-General compromised with this attitude. But if he did, how gravely he would then betray the trust of all those for whom the strict maintenance of such an attitude is their best protection in the world-wide fight for power and influence."

Dag paused, and his hands holding the text of the speech trembled slightly. But he went on. . . .

He would prefer to have the secretary-general's office destroyed on strict adherence to the principles of independence, impartiality and objectivity than drift on the basis of compromise. "That is the choice daily facing the Secretary-General," he said.

Pausing again to stare out at the sea of intent faces, he told them in slow, measured tones that this choice—the choice of compromise versus independence—was also the choice now facing the General Assembly. The decision, he concluded, was in the hands of the member nations.

A thunderous ovation greeted Dag's words. The applause swept through the great hall, then gathered renewed momentum. Seated in the Soviet delegation, Premier Khrushchev bristled with anger, his face crimson and he began to shout and pound the desk in uncontrolled fury.

"I demand the right to reply," he roared again and again as the applause for Dag continued to mount. By this time the entire hall was in an uproar. Assembly President Boland vainly pounded with his gavel for order.

When a semblance of quiet was restored, Khrushchev was given the floor to reply to the Secretary-General. Pointing his stubby finger for emphasis, the Soviet premier angrily declared that the Congo was an incidental matter. The question was a personal as well as a constitutional issue, he maintained. The world had changed drastically since the United Nations had been established. The world organization was now out of date! A billion people lived in socialist countries and another billion lived in neutralist states in Asia and Africa.

"Only one man"—Dag Hammarskjold—interprets and executes the decisions of the Security Council and the General Assembly, Khrushchev charged. There are "no saints on earth" who could adequately represent and defend the interests of the three political blocs in the world—the Western militarists, the Socialists and the Neutralists, he added.

"Is it not clear whose interests he interprets and executes, whose 'Saint' he is?" the Communist leader stormed. "Mr. Hammarskjold has always been biased with regard to the socialist countries, he has always upheld the interests of the United States and other countries of monopoly capital."

Khrushchev then concluded: "To avoid misinterpretation, I want to affirm that we do not trust Mr. Hammarskjold and cannot trust him. If he himself does not muster up enough courage to resign, so to say, in a chivalrous manner, then we shall draw the necessary conclusions from the situation obtaining."

Dag leaned over and whispered anxiously to Boland to get the floor. Boland shook his head and advised him to wait for the afternoon session.

The explosive meeting was adjourned.

The Secretary-General spent most of his lunch hour preparing a statement which he tucked into his pocket just before rejoining the delegates as they assembled for the afternoon session. The air was even more highly charged than in the morning, and Dag was the center of attention as he walked quietly into the hall and took his seat.

When he got the floor he told the Assembly that he was addressing himself to men who were free of mind. "Only on a scrutiny of truth can a future of peace be built," he said simply.

He pointed out again that the issue at stake was not that of a man but of an institution. "The man does not count, the institution does. A weak or nonexistent executive would mean that the United Nations would no longer be able to serve as an effective instrument for active protection of the interests of those many members who need such protection. The man holding the responsibility as chief executive should leave if he weakens the executive; he should stay if this is necessary for its maintenance."

That issue and that issue alone should be the deciding point, Dag told them. He reminded the assemblage that the Soviet premier had declared that it was not possible to work with him and observed that this might seem to provide a strong reason for him to resign. But he also noted that the Russians wanted to replace him with a body of three which would make it impossible to maintain an effective executive.

"By resigning," he stated in a voice that rose in pitch slightly, "I would, therefore, at the present difficult and dangerous juncture throw the organization to the winds. I have no right to do so . . ."

A vigorous round of applause greeted this declaration. Dag waited for the applause to stop, then went on: ". . . I have no right to do so because I have a responsibility to all those member states for which the organization is of decisive importance, a responsibility which overrides all other considerations.

"It is not the Soviet Union or, indeed, any other big powers who need the UN for their protection; it is all the others. In this sense the organization is first of all *their* organization, and I deeply believe in the wisdom with which they will be able to use it and guide it."

Here he paused once again, took a deep breath and stated simply and unemotionally, "I shall remain in my post. . . ." A resounding roar of approval greeted his words while the Communist bloc delegates, led by Premier Khrushchev, pounded their desks in angry protest.

President Boland banged his gavel and pleaded for order, but it was a long time before the noise died down and Dag was permitted to continue. ". . . I shall remain in my post during the term of my office as a servant of the organization in the interests of all those other nations, as long as they wish me to do so."

Then the Secretary-General delivered his concluding words. He spoke with quiet restraint, yet there was a ringing quality to them: "It is very easy to resign; it is not so easy to stay on. It is very easy to bow to the wish of a big power. It is another matter to resist. As is well known to all members of this Assembly, I have done so before on many occasions and in many directions.

"If it is the wish of those nations who see in the organization their best protection in the present world, I shall now do so again."

Even as Dag finished, the delegates were on their feet, applauding wildly in a standing ovation. It was the most emotional demonstration in the United Nations' fifteen-year history. Experienced UN observers later confessed they had never seen anything to equal it. Delegates rushed up to Dag to congratulate him, and flashbulbs popped as news photographers sought to record the historic moment.

The walls of the domed Assembly Hall shook as each round of applause set off a new wave. President Boland, realizing that any effort to restore order was futile, simply gave up and leaned back in his chair smiling.

The ovation, which dwarfed even that given Dag in the morning, told the story more effectively than any vote of support for him could have done. The Secretary-General—acting as spokesman for all the people of the world—had stood up to the challenge of the mighty Soviet superpower and had triumphed. The glum look on Khrushchev's face and those of the other Communist delegates was eloquent testimony to Dag's rousing victory.

When the Assembly finally adjourned, Dag wearily returned to his office to sign some papers and to inform his secretary that he was going home early. It was one of the few times in his life that he felt physically and emotionally spent.

He had intended going directly to his apartment, but on the way down in the elevator he changed his mind and paused for a short time in the UN Meditation Room, situated on the ground floor of the General Assembly Building. It was a room of stillness whose dominating feature was a huge block of Swedish iron. A single shaft of light illuminated the great rectangular slab of metal.

For several minutes the Secretary-General sat in silent contemplation, trying to forget the crowded events of the day. Finally he got up and walked slowly to the door, pausing only

to glance at the black marble plaque at the entrance to the room
with its familiar words which he himself had written:

THIS IS A ROOM DEVOTED
TO PEACE
AND THOSE WHO ARE
GIVING THEIR LIVES
FOR PEACE

IT IS A ROOM OF
QUIET WHERE ONLY
THOUGHT SHOULD SPEAK

Later that night Dag was amazed to learn that he had been
invited to a party at the Soviet Embassy the following evening!
The invitation had actually arrived that morning, but he had
been convinced it was a mistake and had asked an aide to check
on it. When the telephone rang in his apartment and he was
told that the invitation had not been sent in error, he could
hardly believe his ears. Particularly since Khrushchev himself
was to be the host!

The next evening he drove up to the Soviet Embassy at Park
Avenue near Sixty-eighth Street. The building was crowded with
Communist and non-Communist delegates and other guests. He
tried to remain inconspicuous, but Premier Khrushchev himself
spotted him and rushed over to embrace him in a crushing bear
hug. For the rest of the evening the Communist leader refused
to let him out of his sight and kept plying him with toast after
toast. In between drinks, Khrushchev slapped him on the back
a dozen times and told him jokes as if the events of the previous
day had never taken place.

Even the other Communists were confused by this display
of good fellowship. One asked the Soviet Premier in a whisper
why he was being so friendly to the Secretary-General. Khrushchev roared with laughter and replied so others could hear, "I
see you are ignorant of the tradition of the Caucasian mountain

people of Russia. It tells you that when an enemy is inside your
house, sharing your bread and salt, you should always treat him
with the greatest hospitality. But as soon as he is outside your
door, it is all right to slit his throat!"

A little more than a week later, Khrushchev prepared to leave
the United States. In a farewell address to the General Assembly he declared, "I am not fighting Mr. Hammarskjold personally. We have met. We have had very courteous and pleas-
ant conversations. In fact, I consider that Mr. Hammarskjold
is beholden to me. When he was my guest on the Black Sea,
he exploited me; I rowed him around and he has not paid back
in kind. So, as representatives will see, this is not a personal
matter."

Then Dag, requesting the floor for a reply, turned to the
Soviet leader and said, "I was very happy to hear that Mr.
Khrushchev has good memories of the time when I had the
honor to be rowed by him on the Black Sea. I have not, as he
said, been able to reply in kind. But my promise to do so stands,
and I hope the day will come when he can avail himself of this
offer. For if he did I am sure that he would discover that I know
how to row—following only my own compass."

The closing months of 1960 and the early part of 1961 was
a busy and difficult time for Dag. While violence in the Congo
had been halted as a result of the presence of United Nations
troops, a political settlement seemed as remote as ever. The
major problem was the presence of Belgian and other foreign
mercenaries in secessionist Katanga who were advising against
unification with the central Congolese government and encouraging resistance to the United Nations.

Finally, on February 21, the patience of the Security Council
was exhausted. It passed a resolution urging measures to get
rid of all foreign military personnel and mercenaries not under
the United Nations command.

The resolution was sent to Moise Tshombe. As the months
passed, however, the Katanganese failed to carry out its provi-

sions. Therefore, on August 24 the central Congolese government called on the United Nations to help expel all non-Congolese officers and mercenaries serving in the Katanganese forces.

On September 12 Dag left New York for the Congo to take personal charge of the effort to negotiate a settlement. When he stepped off the plane at Léopoldville, he learned that fighting had broken out between mercenary-led Katanganese units and the United Nations troops in Stanleyville.

After several days of futile attempts to initiate discussions with Moise Tshombe, a message was gotten through to the Katanganese leader. He agreed to a meeting with the Secretary-General in Ndola, Northern Rhodesia.

On the afternoon of September 17, Dag and his party of aides took off from Ndjili Airport in Léopoldville and headed for Ndola to try to arrange a cease-fire with the leader of the secessionist province.

Chapter Eighteen

TRAGEDY IN THE JUNGLE

The shocking news that Dag Hammarskjold's plane was missing en route to Ndola stunned the whole world. As the morning wore on, an armada of search planes winged over the primeval jungles of the Congo and Rhodesia, frantically searching for a clue.

In United Nations headquarters, delegates and members of the Secretariat tried to bolster each other's spirits as they waited hopefully for news from the African bush that the Secretary-General was safe.

The news never came.

At three o'clock in the afternoon of September 19—Dag's plane was now fifteen hours overdue—a Rhodesian pilot radioed the control tower at Ndola to report tragic news. He had spotted a fire-blackened patch of trees and charred wreckage in the bush six miles from Ndola. The United Nations plane had crashed; there was no sign of life.

A party of searchers left at once to hack their way through the thick jungle. When they reached the scene of the crash they found a long scar of broken trees and torn up dirt where the plane had rammed through. All that remained of the main fuselage was a gray circle of ashes, and the only recognizable part of the craft was an engine cowling that had been hurled sixty yards away. Sifting through the fragments, the searchers found fourteen bodies, charred beyond recognition. A few yards away they came upon another body, almost untouched and immediately recognizable. It was the Secretary-General.

In death, Dag Hammarskjold's face was a mask of repose and serenity. Nearby was a copy of a book that he had brought with him from the United States. It was a *Life of Christ*, printed in French.

One passenger was still alive, though badly burnt. He was Sergeant Harold M. Julian, a United Nations security guard who was immediately rushed back for medical care. Though only partly conscious, he later gave a confused account of the tragedy. Just after the Swedish pilot had received landing instructions from Ndola tower, the Secretary-General had ordered the pilot to stay aloft and alter his course. Beyond that, Sergeant Julian was unable to supply additional information. He died several days later.

When confirmation of Dag's death reached UN headquarters in New York, a high-ranking Secretariat official turned away from the teletype machine and said dully to a colleague, "I suppose we should lower the flag." The other nodded tearfully.

As the news spread from floor to floor, pale and shaken employees and delegates gathered in the lobbies and corridors. Many sobbed unashamedly. The scene was repeated in United Nations outposts and in many foreign ministries throughout the world.

Meanwhile, back in the heart of the African bush the body of the fifty-six-year-old Secretary-General was removed from the scene of the catastrophe and carried to the small St. Andrews' United Church of Ndola. There Dag Hammarskjold lay in state. His slight body rested in a mahogany casket which was draped with the blue-and-yellow flag of Sweden and surrounded by a sea of fresh flowers.

Four sentries stood at rigid attention as diplomats and others who had managed to reach the remote outpost entered quietly to pay their last respects. One of the visitors was Moise Tshombe, whom Dag had come to see. He walked in, placed a wreath of white lilies on the casket and stood motionless for a long, silent moment. Then he bowed and left the church, saying almost tearfully in French, "It is a sad thing. . . ."

When identification of the others who had died with the Secretary-General was completed the names formed a tragic list. In addition to Dag and Sergeant Julian, they included: Heinrich A. Wieschhoff, adviser and specialist on African affairs; Vladimir Fabry, an aide assigned to the United Nations Operation in the Congo; William Ranallo, personal aide to the Secretary-General; Miss Alice Lalande, a UN secretary; Sergeant Serge L. Barrau, a security officer; Sergeant Francis Eivers, a UN investigator; and two Swedish soldiers stationed in Léopoldville: Warrant Officer S. O. Hjelte and Private P. E. Persson.

The Swedish crew of the plane consisted of Captains Per Hallonquist and Nils-Eric Aahreus, pilots, Second Pilot Lars Litton, Flight Engineer Nils Goran Wilhelmsson, Air Purser Harald Noork and Radio Operator Karl Erik Rosen.

What had caused the accident? Was it due to mechanical failure, pilot error—or foul play? In the days following the tragedy, many dark suspicions were voiced. But no one could come forward with an answer.

Investigators assigned by the United Nations and the government of Rhodesia did their best to ascertain the reason for the crash. During the official inquiries some observers claimed to have seen "a great flash of light" on the night of the accident. Others said they had spotted a second, smaller plane flying near a large transport in the approximate vicinity where Dag's plane had gone down. However, with the death of Sergeant Julian it appeared likely that the true circumstances surrounding the tragedy would remain a mystery forever.

In the days following the death of the Secretary-General, the cease-fire for which he had sacrificed his life was successfully arranged between the United Nations and Katanga Province. Then, on September 28, 1961, Dag's body was flown to his native land. Upon arrival in Stockholm, the flag-draped casket was taken to Uppsala in late afternoon. As it entered the university town where Dag had spent his boyhood, the bells of ancient Uppsala Cathedral began to toll while thousands stood silently in the streets as the cortege slowly passed through the city. More than eight thousand people filed past the coffin that evening to pay their last respects to their countryman who had been the spokesman for all the people of the world.

Back in Stockholm more than two hundred and fifty thousand Swedes paid tribute in a silent, moving spectacle. In four seemingly never-ending columns, men, women and children streamed into the city's famous old Gaerdet parade ground where a huge portrait of Dag had been raised. At the head of each column marched Swedish United Nations soldiers carrying the flags of the member nations of the UN. They marched toward the portrait in dead silence, and the only sounds came from the slogging of feet and muffled drums. Hundreds carried flaming torches, and as the columns marched they converged on a single goal—the portrait of the late Secretary-General. When the parade ground was jammed to absolute capacity, a little ceremony was held and two military bands played mournful music.

The next day United Nations leaders, diplomats and members of foreign governments from every corner of the world gathered in Uppsala Cathedral for the state funeral which had been decreed for Dag. Among those in attendance were King Gustaf and Queen Louise of Sweden.

The coffin, draped with a Swedish flag, lay in front of an altar bedecked with flowers and surrounded by six tall candles. Four flag bearers stood at attention as Archbishop Emeritus Erling Eidem, former head of the State Lutheran Church, began to speak.

He spoke simply and movingly. "To serve," he said, "is the answer to the always-so-disturbing questions of the meaning and the fulfillment of our life on earth . . . Dag Hammarskjold was a faithful son of his fatherland, the devoted servant of all mankind."

Now the casket was lifted gently and placed on a catafalque carriage normally reserved for the kings of Sweden. As the vehicle moved slowly along the road, ten thousand people massed along the way in silent farewell.

At the cemetery, Dag's brothers, Bo and Sten, and his nephew Knut bowed their heads in silent grief. Finally, the coffin was lowered into the family grave where his father, mother and brother Ake lay.

Dag Hammarskjold had reached his final resting place.

In the days and weeks that followed, tributes were paid by the leading statesmen of the world. "His name will be treasured high among the peacemakers of history," President John F. Kennedy declared.

Honors by the dozen were conferred posthumously. At United Nations headquarters a new six-story Hammarskjold Library was dedicated in his memory. And a Hammarskjold Memorial Scholarship fund was established by the UN Correspondents Association to provide scholarships in the United States for young journalists from underdeveloped nations. Several countries, including the United States and Sweden, announced the issuance of Dag Hammarskjold memorial stamps.

But perhaps the greatest of all tributes came from the Nobel Peace Prize Committee. Less than five weeks after his death, it named him a posthumous winner of the Nobel Peace Prize for 1961.

Since the death of Dag Hammarskjold, the United Nations to which he gave his life has had to meet many challenges. As the months and years pass, it will face many more. Perhaps never before in history had one single man played so central a role in the cause of world peace or been so sorely missed.

Yet his presence continues to live as a symbol of the tireless efforts that mankind must make for its continued survival in a nuclear age. Through the principles and convictions he set down for the future, Dag helped illumine a path for nations to follow in their quest for peace based on human dignity and international order. Thus the name of Dag Hammarskjold has entered history—and history reserves its highest honors for the heroes of peace.

BIBLIOGRAPHY

Claude, Inis L., Jr. *Swords into Plowshares: The Problems and Progress of International Organization.* New York: Random House, 1956.

Coyle, David Cushman. *The United Nations and How It Works.* New York: Columbia University Press, 1955.

Haines, C. Grove and Hoffman, Ross J. S. *The Origins and Background of the Second World War.* New York: Oxford University Press, 1943.

Hammarskjold, Dag. *The International Civil Servant in Law and in Fact.* London: Oxford University Press, 1961.

Hammarskjold, Dag. "Introduction to the Annual Report of the Secretary-General on the Work of the Organization, June 16, 1960–June 15, 1961." *United Nations Review,* September, 1961.

Hammarskjold, Dag. "The Positive Role of the United Nations in a Split World: Introduction to the Fifteenth Annual Report of the Secretary-General to the General Assembly, August 31, 1960." *United Nations Review,* October, 1960.

Holden, David. "Congo Close-Up of the U.N." *The New York Times Magazine,* October 22, 1961.

Kugelmass, J. Alvin. *Ralph II. Bunche: Fighter for Peace.* New York: Julian Messner, Inc., 1952.

Lash, Joseph P. *Dag Hammarskjold: Custodian of the Brushfire Peace.* New York: Doubleday & Company, 1961.

Levin, Meyer. "Sage Who Inspired Hammarskjold." *The New York Times Magazine,* December 3, 1961.

Lie, Trygve. *In the Cause of Peace.* New York: The Macmillan Company, 1954.

Lodge, Henry Cabot. "A Colleague's Salute." *Life,* September 29, 1961.

Miller, Richard I. *Dag Hammarskjold and Crisis Diplomacy.* New York: Oceana Publications, Inc., 1961.

Schwebel, Stephen M. *The Secretary-General of the United Nations.* Cambridge, Mass.: Harvard University Press, 1962.

Sprout, Harold and Margaret, editors. *Foundations of National Power.* Princeton, New Jersey: Princeton University Press, 1945.

"The Death of Secretary-General Dag Hammarskjold." *United Nations Review,* October, 1961.

"United Nations, Battlefield of Peace." *Time,* September 29, 1961.

INDEX

185

About the Author

I. E. LEVINE is a native New Yorker. He graduated from DeWitt Clinton High School and enrolled at the City College of New York as a physics major. After working on the college newspaper for two years, he was convinced that he wanted to be a writer and changed his major to English and the social sciences. He received his degree, went to work in the public relations department at City College, and in 1954 was appointed to his present post of Director of Public Relations. He has written many articles for national magazines, is co-author of several adult books and well known for his biographies for young people. He and his family make their home in Kew Gardens Hills, Long Island.